"Doctors have needed this book for years. It is well researched, comprehensive, and accurate. Better yet, it is jam packed with practical advice and contact information for patients and their families. I can't think of a more valuable resource for a doctor to prescribe or people to read. If you want to show someone you care, forgo the cards and flowers. Give this book. It will make a world of difference."

DAVID L. STEVENS, M.D.
EXECUTIVE DIRECTOR, CHRISTIAN MEDICAL AND DENTAL ASSOCIATIONS

"*Life on Hold* skillfully blends the poignancy of the authors' personal journey through illness with practical ways of coping with the life changes that inevitably come. Focusing on the reality of God's comfort and guidance in difficult times, this book is a hopeful, helpful resource for clinicians as well as patients and family members. As a clinical psychologist, I highly recommend this book to both professionals and nonprofessionals."

DANIEL L. HAFFEY, PSY.D.
LICENSED PSYCHOLOGIST, PRIVATE PRACTICE
FREDERICK, MARYLAND

"*Life on Hold* offers powerful and penetrating insight into the journey of grief. Interlaced with the love and compassion brought about by painful personal experience, it offers practical guidance that affords both understanding and solace to the grieving heart. Moving and profound, this book is filled with pain and triumph. But most of all, it overflows with the wisdom and comfort found when people turn to God in times of personal crisis.

"*Life on Hold* will prove invaluable to professionals and laypeople alike in both training and practice. More importantly, it will help individuals and families understand and master the challenges facing illness, death, and dying. As a hospital chaplain and bereavement counselor, I highly recommend this book."

REV. ROBERT E. STEINKE
HOSPITAL CHAPLAIN AND MANAGER OF PASTORAL CARE
FREDERICK, MARYLAND

Life on Hold

FINDING HOPE
IN THE FACE OF
SERIOUS ILLNESS

Laurel Seiler Brunvoll and
David G. Seiler

Multnomah®Publishers *Sisters, Oregon*

LIFE ON HOLD
published by Multnomah Publishers, Inc.

© 2001 by Laurel Seiler Brunvoll and David G. Seiler
International Standard Book Number: 9781590528273

Cover image by Jeremy Walker/Tony Stone Images

Scripture quotations are from:
New American Standard Bible © 1960, 1977 by the Lockman Foundation

The Holy Bible, New International Version (NIV) © 1973, 1984 by International Bible Society, used by permission of Zondervan Publishing House

Multnomah is a trademark of Multnomah Publishers, Inc., and is registered in the U.S. Patent and Trademark Office.
The colophon is a trademark of Multnomah Publishers, Inc.

For information:
MULTNOMAH PUBLISHERS, INC.
POST OFFICE BOX 1720
SISTERS, OREGON 97759

Library of Congress Cataloging–in–Publication Data:
Brunvoll, Laurel Seiler. Life on hold : finding hope in the face of serious illness / Laurel Seiler Brunvoll and David G. Seiler. p.cm. ISBN 9781590528273 (pbk.)
1. Terminally ill–Religious life. 2. Terminally ill–Family relationships. I. Seiler, David G. II. Title. BV4910.B78 2001 248.8'61–dc21 00-013149

01 02 03 04 0146651086 6 5 4 3 2 1 0

This book is dedicated to

Nancy Sara Seiler,

faithful, dedicated servant of God
and loving wife, mother, and grandmother.

Table of Contents

Acknowledgments

There are many, many people we want to thank for their important roles in this five-year labor of love. Please forgive us if we've left anyone out.

We want to thank our beloved wife and mother, Nancy Seiler, for her inspiring example of how to walk with Jesus when life gets hard.

We thank all our friends and family. Your support and encouragement made a world of difference, and many of you shared your experiences with us. Rebecca, you're not only a sister, but also a friend for life. Holly and Alden Estep, you are like family to us. Howard and Arline Brunvoll, we could not ask for better in-laws. Thank you for everything, including treating the boys to a two-week adventure at your house while we finished the book.

Gaithersburg Presbyterian Church members, thank you for your incredible love and support during our darkest days. Thank you: Blaine Smith, for great advice when we first began writing; Chris Platt, for your critical analysis and insight; Anna Joyce, for your keen eye; Donna Roop and Donna Nordquist for being true friends; and Jolene, Rachel, and Alice Catherine Mutchler, and Kinsley Wilde, for being responsible and fun baby-sitters.

We want to thank the many health-care professionals and pastors who took the time to share words of wisdom, lessons learned, and stories from their own lives with us. We especially acknowledge: Chaplain Bob, Dan Haffey, Mary Raymer, Mark Tindle, Butch Hardman, Joe Nilsen, Faye Serene, and David Stevens.

We want to thank our agent, Mike Petersen, for seeing the importance of our message and successfully finding our book a home.

We appreciate the eagerness to help and the kindness of everyone at Multnomah. We especially thank Bill Jensen for his encouragement and Judith St. Pierre, our editor, for her guidance and wisdom.

A special thanks from Laurel: Joshua and Michael, thank you for believing in me and giving me some alone time to write. Steven, this book would never have gone anywhere without your overwhelming support and the sacrifices you made to help me.

Most of all, we thank God for His hand in this book. From concept to fruition, He guided and directed us. May He use it for His glory!

Introduction

I have been thrust out of the world, which we all think is so important and found myself standing on the edge of eternity. There the view is very much different.

Because you have picked up this book, chances are that you have entered an incredibly difficult time in your life. Either you or someone you love has been ushered into a new world, a place where nothing feels or looks the same. Everything has changed forever, and your life is on hold as you struggle to survive physically, emotionally, and spiritually.

Maybe tomorrow I will find out what is wrong with me. I have such strange reactions. I am not really afraid, yet I can't help think what if there is something seriously wrong with me.

January 1990 was the first time my mother, Nancy Seiler, wondered if something was physically wrong with her. In February her doctor discovered a large mass in her abdominal area, and a month later she had surgery for metastasized ovarian cancer. From March through July she underwent chemotherapy treatments that caused many painful side effects. After the last treatment, she was basically free of symptoms for one year.

In September 1991, however, the cancer returned. It had spread to her liver, and we thought that she would die shortly. But on December 20, after two months of chemotherapy treatments, she was accepted into an experimental program at the National Institutes of Health (NIH) in Bethesda, Maryland. Every three weeks she returned to the NIH hospital for a twenty-four-hour infusion of Taxol. All treatments were administered in intensive care because the chemicals caused her heart to stop. These treatments continued until December 1992.

Mom enjoyed another clinical remission for almost a year, but at the end of November 1993, the cancer returned. She tried another experimental treatment, but it was particularly harsh and left her with little quality of life. At that point, she decided not to have more chemotherapy treatments because none of them promised much more than a small probability of remission. She felt that it was more important to enjoy what time was left than to extend her misery.

In January 1994 the NIH staff told her that she had six months to live. Without treatments, she had a good quality of life until July. Then in August she had an intestinal blockage. After a hospitalization to stabilize her, she was admitted to a hospice program. She died at home on September 6, 1994.

Two and a half years after my mom died, my father and coauthor, David Seiler, was diagnosed with renal cell carcinoma. He underwent a radical nephrectomy in January 1997. Thankfully, he has had no signs of recurrence.

When my dad and I look back over those years of agony and worry, we clearly see God's hand moving in our lives as He helped and encouraged us. When my mom first became ill, we prayed that she would be able to see my sister, Rebecca, get married. She did. We prayed that her dream to become a grandmother would come true. It did. We prayed for her to have some good quality of life. She did. We also prayed for strength, hope, and peace—and again God answered us.

> *"And I will turn their mourning into joy; and will comfort them, and give them joy for their sorrow"* (Jeremiah 31:13). *I'm not sure if this promise is to me or to my husband and children, but I feel that it is pertinent to our case.*

This book has been on our hearts and minds for years. It reflects not only our own experiences, but also nearly five years of research and interviews with health-care professionals and caregivers, patients, and family members. We feel honored to share what we've learned, but more than anything else, we want to offer you words of hope and encouragement. Even though no one can understand the depths of what you are going through today and what you may face tomorrow, we hope you find this book a companion that will help and comfort you on your journey.

Life on Hold provides up-to-date information on the emotional, physical, relational, psychological, and spiritual side effects of physical illness. One of our goals in writing it was to find the most creative, resourceful ways people can overcome the obstacles they encounter when they are dealing with a serious illness. Thus, it offers patients, family members, caregivers, and friends practical suggestions and useful advice for getting through each new day. It is also a helpful resource for pastors, lay and professional counselors, and anyone who is interested in ministering to people struggling with serious illness. Health-care workers and mental health practitioners will find it beneficial in their practice as they seek to identify better with their patients.

Another, larger, goal of this book was to help you find hope in the face of serious illness. It's one thing to learn coping methods and strategies and quite another to be filled with peace and hope in the face of severe adversity. Therefore, we have combined biblical truths with practical information throughout the book. Our desire is for you to find meaning, purpose, and peace in the midst of pain, suffering, and even death.

The book is divided into three parts: "A Bend in the Road," "Making the Turn," and "Journey's End." Each part deals with a different stage of coping with serious illness. The first two concentrate on living fully in the face of serious illness, while the third shows how living intentionally can maximize the spiritual and emotional aspects of death for both the dying and the living. Which section you read first may depend on where you are in your journey. At the end of each chapter is a practical application section designed to help you dig deeper and put into practice the things you learned from the chapter.

Although the book has two authors, for ease of reading, mine is the narrating voice. My father and I share the thoughts and opinions expressed in this book, but our different roles and experiences provide unique perspectives and a variety of insights. My mother's voice is heard through her journal entries, which she told us to use however we wished. Undated and arranged topically, they appear throughout the book to illustrate how one patient felt and thought as she lived with a serious illness. We have reproduced the entries just as she wrote them.

No matter what your circumstances are right now, know that God will take care of you and your family. He is more powerful than any illness and wants only the best for you. Lean on Him as your ultimate Comforter. He will give you all the hope, peace, and strength you need for your journey—every step of the way.

As I have fought cancer for the last four years, I have learned that life is meant to transform us into persons qualified to rule in heaven with Christ. How many people see their time on earth in the eternal perspective?

PART I

A BEND
IN THE ROAD

I used to envision the worst that could happen so that I would be ready for it when it came. This is self-defeating, for rather than prepare you, such an exercise disturbs the peace of the present for it anticipates an evil that is not yet a reality and for which God has not provided strength.

Save me, O God,
For the waters have come up to my soul.
I have sunk in deep mire,
and there is no foothold;
I have come into deep waters,
and a flood overflows me.
I am weary with my crying;
My throat is parched;
My eyes fail while I wait for my God.

PSALM 69:1–3

———————

What will help when, sudden as a shell screaming out of the night,
one of the great crashing dispensations bursts in your life,
and leaves an emptiness where there had been a home,
a tumbled ruin of your ordered ways,
a heart so sore you wonder how it holds together?

JOHN GOSSIP

ONE

As If a Portal Opened

T he middle-aged man sat staring at a corner of the waiting room. His hands fidgeted above the newspapers, which lay unread in his lap. Too much time had elapsed since the surgery began early that morning.

"Why aren't they done yet?" he mumbled to himself, glancing at the clock.

At the end of the room, a door opened, and two doctors approached him, motioning him into the consultation room.

"I'm sorry, Mr. Seiler," one of them said. "Your wife has cancer, and it's spread throughout her abdominal area. We need your permission to hand over the rest of the surgery to oncologists. There's a team down the hallway, ready to begin. All you have to do is say the word."

What did they just say? he wondered. *Is she going to die?*

Silently, my dad stepped out of the room reserved for bad news and shuffled toward my sister and the associate pastor of his church, who had been waiting with him all morning. Wave after wave of sobs engulfed him, and for fifteen minutes he was unable to speak. Rebecca hugged him the entire time, squeezing him harder and harder, as if through effort alone she could make the nightmare go away.

When he went to the hospital cafeteria two hours later, my dad hurried through the line, putting only a few items on his tray. *Why are there no tables with one chair?* he asked himself. Finally he slid into a booth, alone. *Everything is gone—all my hopes and dreams,* he said to himself. *Where are you, God, anyway?*

In that moment of anguish, he felt a tap on his shoulder. He looked up to see the head pastor of his church, a six-foot-tall Scottish minister whose deep care and concern for God's people shone from his blue eyes. His comforting presence was God's answer to my father's prayer.

Down the hall in the recovery room, my mother was coming out of the anesthetic. In her journal, she described what she felt when she awakened from the difficult surgery.

"Wake up. Wake up and become the person I meant you to be when you became Mine," said the Lord. But I could not hear Him. All I heard was a voice saying, "Nancy, you have cancer. They found cancer on your ovaries during surgery."

I tried to form a thought—what did this message mean? But it was too soon because the anesthetic had not yet cleared, and I was left only with the words hanging in my mind. If only I could stay in this lovely state where nothing caused a riffle of emotion, but all too soon the fog lifted and reality leaped into my consciousness. I entered a living hell as I discovered strange tubes inserted into my chest and nose and remembered those words spoken through the darkness, penetrating like a poisoned dart into the soft underside of my mind.

"Why did I not die on the table?" I thought. "Is there anything left to live for?" My answer came as my family entered, trying to look cheerful in a room pregnant with death.

FINDING OUT

Do you remember the exact words the physician used when he gave you or your loved one his diagnosis? People who have been in that situation almost always remember them vividly. They recall where they were and what time of day it was. They have no trouble remembering the exact instant when everything changed—the moment after which life never looked the same again, no matter how many days, weeks, months, or even years have passed.

The surgeon's knife causes pain when it slices into a patient's body. Strong medication can dull or erase that hurt. But there's no anesthesia to numb the soul-searing pain people feel when they hear the words "You have cancer or multiple sclerosis, AIDS/HIV, Parkinson's disease, Alzheimer's disease, ALS (Lou Gehrig's disease), or _____."

The words that came to me that day brought me to my knees. I have been dealt a severe blow and am not sure I will ever smile again.

Reactions to a diagnosis will vary, depending upon your personality, personal and family circumstances, philosophy of life, and the severity of the diagnosis. Response to stress is an extremely personalized process, and your reaction to the news may be very different from another person in the same situation. Mary Raymer, a social worker who has worked with the seriously ill and their families since 1978, says that individual reactions to a diagnosis of serious illness range from one extreme to another. "I've seen the whole gamut of responses," she says. "Some people feel a calmness now that their illness has been diagnosed; others experience tremendous anxiety, anger, and fear. Much depends on who we are to begin with and on our cultural or family backgrounds."[1]

How the diagnosis is shared will greatly affect your response.

Psychologist Daniel L. Haffey says that there is a huge difference between a physician who gives the clinical news with compassion and one who dumps it in an insensitive way. "If you have a physician who knows how to frame the medical news, you can often handle it better," Dr. Haffey says. "But," he adds, "being compassionate does not mean lying to a patient about known facts."[2]

"Patients should listen," says Dr. Elise C. Kohn, "but should have someone else there to listen, too. Having two listeners is important. Tape recorders don't help because they don't record the face of the speaker." She adds that it is important to get written copies of information relayed in conversations. Informed consents and descriptions of medical conditions have to be reviewed and approved, so they are usually written in language that is clear and easy to understand.[3]

Although reactions to diagnoses vary, patients and caregivers have many symptoms in common during the first few weeks as they struggle to comprehend the severity of the illness. The most obvious symptom is grief.

The *Encyclopedia of Death* defines grief as "the highly personal and subjective set of responses that an individual makes to a real, perceived, or anticipated loss."[4] It has also been defined as the feeling of being robbed of something valued.[5] People value health, and when robbed of it, they grieve. People value the life of a loved one, and when it is threatened or taken, they grieve.

In *A Grief Observed*, C. S. Lewis describes the feelings that accompanied his own grief over the death of his wife.

> Tonight all the hells of young grief have opened again; the mad words, the bitter resentment, the fluttering in the stomach, the nightmare unreality, the wallowed-in tears. For in grief nothing "stays put." One keeps on emerging from a phase, but it always recurs. Round and round. Everything repeats. Am I going in circles, or dare I hope I am on a spiral?[6]

Raymer says that people with a serious illness grieve something they've lost because they know that it's impossible to go back to the way things were before they were diagnosed.

TELLING OTHERS

Very soon after the diagnosis has been made, the need arises to give the news to family and friends.

If you are having a hard time even thinking about your illness, it will of course be difficult for you to say much about it to anyone. That's okay. Don't push yourself. However, you may want to keep in the back of your mind that your family and friends are concerned about you and that they will learn of the diagnosis sooner or later. Getting the situation out in the open quickly may lower your stress level and allow other people to express their love for you.

What you say when people ask you about your illness or prognosis is a personal decision. It will probably depend upon who they are, how well you know them, and the amount of information you feel comfortable giving them. "It depends upon your social circumstances, the relationships you have, and your personality," says Dr. Wendy Schlessel Harpham, who was diagnosed with disseminated lymphoma a few years ago. "If you tend to share and have people with whom you can share, you will probably get much-needed support by sharing your news. If you tend to be very private and independent, you will probably involve the minimum number of people in your new situation."[7]

It is often too difficult or not even feasible for the patient to tell everyone who would want to know about the diagnosis. In fact, the patient may still be under anesthesia and unable to hear or understand what has happened. For these reasons, a family member or a very close friend of the family usually gives the news to the outside world. Are there ways to make this difficult task easier?

If you know that you are going to have surgery or diagnostic tests, it may be helpful for you and your immediate family to decide in advance who will be responsible for communicating the results to whom. For example, I was hundreds of miles away when my mom underwent surgery, so my dad was responsible for keeping me informed. I, in turn, would tell my husband and my in-laws of the outcome, and they would inform other relatives, friends, coworkers, and neighbors. This kind of network helps lessen the burden on you, the patient.

As the news spreads, how can you and your family deal with all the calls that pour in from well-wishers? You cannot possibly return all of them, and you may even find yourself resenting all the inquiries because you simply don't want to talk or just don't know what to say. One family's solution was to record a message informing callers of the patient's basic health status and telling them that they appreciated their calls but that they could not return them right then. This should not discourage friends or family members from calling, however, because they can leave a "thinking of you" message. If you are one of the callers, consider saying that you don't expect a return call.

Giving someone bad news is never easy, but you can start by passing along only information that you can verify. This may mean that you have little to say because you know only the basics. Leave it at that until you learn more. Do not embellish the facts, and do not add your own suppositions to the story.

A word of caution: It is imperative to follow the wishes of the patient. If he* does not want *anyone* to know certain things until a later date, you *must* respect that wish. When in doubt, a loved one should always speak with the patient first. Ask: "What do you want me to tell others?" "How much do you want me to say?" and "How soon should I say it?"

* For ease of reading, we have used male pronouns to refer to both males and females.

DEALING WITH THE DIAGNOSIS

It's hard to predict how someone will respond to a particular crisis. What is important to remember is that reactions that differ from those of other family members or friends are perfectly okay.

When Mom was diagnosed, I wished that someone would have sat down with me and said, "I think that what you're feeling is perfectly normal." When Dad was diagnosed two years after Mom's death, the actions of a close friend told me what I needed to hear.

Shortly after a visit to China, my dad came down with a low-grade fever. It persisted for three weeks. At first, doctors said, "Don't worry, it's just a flu virus." Then he went to a specialist in infectious diseases, and she put him in the hospital to check his blood for malaria. Instead of malaria, Dad had a large, malignant tumor in one of his kidneys. In fact, his right kidney was swollen to more than four times the size of his left one.

At 7 A.M. the next morning, I picked up the phone to call my friend and tell her the news.

"It's just me," I croaked when I heard her voice.

"So, do you know what's wrong with your dad?" she asked.

"It's really bad," I managed to say before I started to cry. "He has kidney cancer."

Her only response was, "Oh, no!" Then she started to cry, too.

Maybe my friend thought that she wasn't helping me very much because she was crying and couldn't talk. Maybe she thought that she should have said something eloquent and encouraging. Maybe she thought that she should have been more positive and uplifting.

But her tears were the most beautiful gift. She hurt enough for my dad and me to cry, and she cared enough to let her emotions show. Isn't that what it is all about? Her tears washed away some of my pain that morning.

Although the grieving process is complicated and reactions differ, there are common responses that can be divided, however loosely, into four categories: emotional, behavioral, physical, and mental.[8]

Emotional

Susan Curry recalls her reaction when her mother was diagnosed with breast cancer:

> When I first found out that the lump my mom had was malignant, I was shocked and numb. I found myself moving from the position of "It will never happen to anyone in my family" to the reality that someone in my family had cancer. I immediately associated the disease with death and went into denial—thinking that God would never allow that to happen. I tried to focus on the positive—treatments, etc.—willing the cancer to be cured and to be a strong support for my mother and the rest of my family.

Denial is a major issue when people learn about a serious illness. "It's almost as if they didn't hear what was said because they want to block it out," Haffey says. He points out that denial can be a good defense mechanism in the short term because it can protect people from the shock of what has happened. In this case, it slowly subsides as reality seeps in. Denial becomes a problem only if it persists too long.

Besides denial, you may feel anger, guilt, anxiety, a sense of helplessness, sadness, despair, shock, numbness, self-blame, apathy, loss of pleasure or enjoyment, agitation, irritability, depression, and panic. You may feel lost and yearn for things left undone, for the way life was, or for plans that are no longer feasible.

Irene Pollin says that people who are dealing with a long-term illness need to recognize that they will struggle daily with its emotional impact. "You and your disease are engaged in a psychological tug-of-war, and right now your illness has the upper hand," she observes.[9]

Haffey agrees that long-term illnesses have far-reaching emotional effects. "There is a shrinking of a person's emotional and psychological world. His world and perceptions narrow right down to whatever the traumatic event is, and everything in the periphery drops away."

It's hard to see a future today. I've got to find a solution to the feeling that my life is all locked in.

If any of these emotions make it difficult for you to make health-care decisions or seek medical treatment, you should find a mental health professional to help you work through your adjustment.

Behavioral

"No, I won't be able to make it," I replied. "I…uh…have too much work to do."

I hung up the receiver, feeling no remorse at my lie. *I just want to be alone. Why do I always have to explain myself to everyone anyway?* I sat on the couch and cried.

I remember how I distanced myself from my friends after my mom's surgery and during her first chemotherapy treatments. I am very much a "people person," but at that time I had no desire to spend time with others. Even my relationship with my husband became strained as I tried to pull away. I felt as if no one else could really understand what I was going through, so I preferred to be alone. Perhaps I just needed to feel sorry for myself.

Acting in atypical ways is a reaction to stress. Be aware that you might start behaving very differently than you did before the diagnosis. Possible behavioral changes include frequent or unexplainable mood changes, lethargy, isolation, restlessness, and self-pity.

You could lose your appetite or overeat, become hostile or cynical, or experience increased or decreased libido. You might feel the need to look for someone to blame or, if you are a family member or close friend, the need to talk about your loved one.

Certain extreme behavior patterns might signal unhealthy ways of trying to cover up fears. If you see yourself or someone you love exhibit risk-tasking behavior—having an extramarital affair, abusing alcohol or medications, or even driving unsafely—seek professional help immediately.

Physical

When my dad was in the hospital for tests, I went back to his room with him after he had a CT scan. Almost two hours later his physician walked in.

The truth was etched in ominous lines on her face, and she did not turn away from our questioning gazes. Words catapulted out of her mouth and landed right in the middle of my soul: "I hate to be the one to tell you this, but you have a very large tumor in your kidney. The good news is that you have two kidneys; the bad news is that one must come out."

"No! No!" I cried out. I grabbed my dad. My arms got tingly, my heart pounded, and I felt light-headed. I thought I would pass out and vomit, all at the same time.

That was how I reacted, but there are as many ways to react to bad news as there are people. Some sleep too much or too little, have feelings of heaviness in the chest or tightness in the throat, or get headaches more frequently. You may experience fatigue, muscle tension, tremors and shakes, increased heart rate, dizziness, decreased coordination, gastrointestinal problems, menstruation irregularities, oversensitivity to noise, sexual impotency, decreased immune functioning, or psychosomatic symptoms. Many people cry a great deal, at times unexpectedly.

I have been crying a lot these days—if not on the out-side, I am crying on the inside. I do my best to wish that all of these recent events were only a bad dream and soon I will wake up again. But it will not go away and I know that life will never again be the same.

Mary Raymer says that all the stress-related symptoms a person has experienced throughout life will probably accompany a health crisis. "There is a good chance that these symptoms will intensify," she adds. She also points out that how a person's family of origin taught him to handle grief—whether it minimized or magnified it—will affect how he reacts.

But the physical difficulties are minor in comparison with what has occurred in my mind. I am devastated. Every dream and plan has been destroyed, and the out-look is bleak. All I can think about is how sorry I am that I will not be able to enjoy all that I have antici-pated.

Mental

For an entire year after her diagnosis of myositis, Chris Platt's world was very, very small. "Being disabled is a tremendous amount of work," she says, "and I was really only aware of a very few things. My judgment and analytical capabilities were impaired, and I became emotionally shallow, unable to bond with my newborn or my husband." A year later, she remembers little of that period, as though she had not really "been there."

"From a mental standpoint, you or your loved one are going through a very self-oriented process," says Raymer. "As people try to figure out, 'what does this mean to me,' they will be in their heads a lot."

You could experience episodes of forgetfulness, confusion, or the inability to do even simple things. You might leave routine chores unfinished, be unable to solve problems, or have difficulty making decisions or remembering things. Or you may have upsetting dreams, decreased attention span, slowed thinking, or decreased concentration.

Mental adjustments to a diagnosis of serious illness vary greatly. Some people see the diagnosis as a challenge and maintain an optimistic view of the future, while others become helpless and hopeless, sure the prognosis will inevitably lead to death. Still others are fatalistic and accept the outcome passively. Others simply remain in denial.

> *Low platelets. The doctor is worried and wants me to stay at home all weekend. I am tired. But I must not allow my tiredness to interfere with my ministry. Last night I took a walk and enjoyed the evening and talked to the Lord. I know that I must learn to rejoice continually. My battle is not so much against my disease as against my mind.*

If you have received the diagnosis of a life-threatening illness or walked the road with a loved one who has, what has been your response? The following comments come from people who have been in that situation. They give you an idea of the many different ways people respond to grief. After you have read through them, write out your own response or circle the words or phrases that describe your feelings.

"I've got to get through this."

"I am concerned about my children."

"Total denial—I didn't believe the doctor at first."

"I sat and cried in a restaurant for an hour."

"Overwhelmed with thoughts of him not growing up."

"Mad."

"The horror of mutilation—I wondered if I would be ugly."

"I experienced a lot of guilt about my marriage."

"My heart was breaking."

"I felt so helpless and out of control."

"My whole life is crushed."

"I became so concerned about the state of his soul."

"I couldn't function very well."

"Thinking the end was days away."

"I was immobilized with dread."

"Extreme sadness."

"I was in sort of a daze."

"It was all a mistake."

"It was difficult to see my family's reaction."

"Mad at God."

"I felt surprised and confused."

"I felt sorry for myself."

"Envious of others' lives."

"What a crushing weight upon me."

"I worried about the suffering."

My response is: _____

If you are not in this situation but know that you might face it in the future, what do you think your response would be?_____

_____

It was as if a portal opened, and I was thrust through into a life as unfamiliar with the previous as moving from this planet to another. It was at the same time, unsolicited and could not be stopped.

If you have been diagnosed with a life-threatening illness, your life *has changed forever*. There is no road back. Many things you used to take for granted are now impossible. Raymer suggests that you allow yourself to grieve. Then you'll be ready to renegotiate what can be *now*, instead of focusing on how things were. An entry in my mom's journal reflects a major shift in her response as she adjusted to an overwhelming situation.

> *I have encountered a whole lifetime of new attitudes and feelings and each day brings new revelations and growth. I must never regret this experience. For too long, I had yearned to grow in my spiritual life and was hampered continually by the physical realm.*

Today you may not think it's possible, but there can come a time when you will feel the same. The next few chapters will show you how you can live with hope in the face of serious illness.

———◆———

F

HELPFUL HINTS FOR GETTING THROUGH THE FIRST SEVERAL WEEKS

According to one study, distress from a serious health diagnosis usually peaks about eight to ten weeks after you receive it.[10] The following suggestions will give you, as a patient, and your loved ones, as caregivers, some practical help in the initial period of your crisis.[11]

As the patient, you can:

- Confide in someone about your illness, worries, and fears.
- Allow yourself to feel and express any and all emotions.
- Find out as much as possible about your illness and the treatments available. See chapter 5 and appendix B for places to look.
- Talk with your medical team to find out all your options and their potential side effects.
- Tell your health-care professional how much information you

can or cannot handle. This may change as time goes on.

- Consider speaking with a social worker or counselor about how to deal with a serious illness, especially with the emotional side effects.
- Get as much rest as possible. Even if you have a difficult time sleeping during the day, close your eyes and enjoy some quiet time.
- Accept offers of help from friends and family members, even if you feel you don't really need it. It reinforces their bond with you and allows them to express their own emotions toward you.
- Between visits to doctors, keep a log of symptoms, side effects, and progress, as well as a list of questions to ask them. My mom kept notes on a calendar. She had dates and specifics organized, which made it easier for her to discuss any setbacks with them.

As a family member or friend, you can:

- Be honest and avoid trite sayings like "Don't worry, everything will be fine."
- Spend time with the patient.
- Send flowers or thoughtful cards. (Add a personal note.)
- Refuse to adopt an attitude of false cheeriness ("I'm sure you'll be okay").
- Let the patient decide when he is ready to talk about the illness.
- Say, "I'm here for you."
- Be yourself and act naturally.
- Make eye contact with the patient.
- Listen—really listen.
- Examine your own emotions. If you feel that you could use support, seek out a social worker or counselor to help you sort through them.

- Maintain family routines. Allowing a patient to take responsibility for doing something helpful for the family makes him feel useful and more than "just a patient."
- Follow the patient's lead if you involve yourself in the actual medical care. Be careful not to nag him to take medication or see the doctor.
- Keep lines of communication open so that no family member is left out or overburdened. This is especially critical if your family is spread out across the country.
- Take a break from time to time, but tell the patient what your plans are and who will be available should he need something while you're gone.
- Continue to eat, sleep, and exercise as regularly as possible.
- Talk to a close friend or relative about your own thoughts and feelings.
- Insist on an atmosphere of respect for the patient. Involve him in all decisions about his illness and treatment.
- Between medical appointments, help the patient keep a log of symptoms, side effects, and progress, as well as a list of questions to ask the doctors. This usually will apply to a spouse, parent, son, or daughter.
- Participate in meetings and information gathering only to the extent that the patient wants you to. Again, this probably applies only to immediate family members.
- Remember that your love, in and of itself, can be very comforting to the patient.
- Accompany the patient to a doctor visit or treatment.
- If your loved one shows an interest, share news about your day, current world events, or social interests.

He will cover you with His pinions,
And under His wings you may seek refuge;
His faithfulness is a shield and bulwark.
For He will give His angels charge concerning you,
To guard you in all your ways.
They will bear you up in their hands,
Lest you strike your foot against a stone.

PSALM 91:4, 11–12

F

Faith is the means by which the infirmity of man
lays hold on the infinity of God.

JOHN BLANCHARD

Two

Every Step of the Way

I want to do it myself!" my two-year-old shouted. His lower lip puffed out as he strained to lift a gallon container of milk and dump it into a bowl of cereal. I picked up a towel and stood nearby, waiting for the inevitable.

Our desire to control our lives starts very early. We all want to direct our lives and do things ourselves. Most of us live under the comfortable illusion that we control more in life than we really do—until a crisis strikes. Just as toddlers throw a fit when control is taken from them, seriously ill people deal with powerful emotions when illness makes them feel that they have lost control of their lives.

STRUGGLING WITH LOSS OF CONTROL

I remember the month my mom spent twenty-seven days in the hospital. She had had an extensive recurrence of her ovarian cancer, and large tumors had been found on her liver. Doctors thought that an experimental ICU-administered chemotherapy was the only way to slow down tumor growth, but the treatment did not appear to be going well. It resulted in fevers and infections, which led to repeated and lengthy stays in the hospital.

I was home for two days, then it was back to the hospital because I was neutropenic and had a fever. I've been experiencing a flat stage again. It's almost like I have no feelings, no desires, no nothing. I just lie in my hospital bed and have no desire to do anything (which is why I've written nothing for so long).... My life has once again drawn in on me. I have few outside contacts. If it were not for my family, I would be mostly alone.

Many patients dealing with a serious illness have to spend vast amounts of unwanted and unplanned time in a hospital, homebound, or bedridden. My mom could not stand to stay in the hospital longer than she expected or to remain in isolation at home when low blood counts dictated it. These experiences were emotionally difficult for her because she had no control over them.

Little did I know what I was getting into. All these days in the hospital and I'm not sure what I am to do about further treatments.

Mary Raymer says that those struggling with loss of control may feel abandoned, either by God or whatever philosophy they hold. Oftentimes, they will doubt the goodness of the world, so to speak. They may feel anxiety, anger, depression, low self-esteem, and intense guilt at being a burden to their families. They might withdraw or lash out against those they love in an attempt to gain control of their lives. Other reactions to loss of control are sleeplessness, loss of appetite, becoming passively or actively suicidal, and aggravated symptoms of their illness.

Once again my hair is gone.... I feel I have drifted during the last two weeks. There was just too much hospital, too much to fight. At the very point, when I needed the Lord the most, all I could do was sit (or lie) and not think. My loneliness has increased. I feel so out-of-touch with the rest of the world. Hope has been lost because I no longer feel a part of society—I might as well be dead.

Looking back, I realize just how strong the connection was between my mom's emotional and spiritual state and how she was feeling physically, especially during her "I am totally out of control" times.

This is ridiculous. Here I am back in the hospital with a fever. I have got to get free of the low spirits for surely (1) the Lord knows I'm here and (2) He has a reason that this should be for my good. I'm depressed because I was under the wrong expectations. The doctor said no side effects. Happiness is a choice. If I feel sorry for myself, then I will be miserable and so will everyone around me. The Lord can lift my spirits.

Yet dealing with the feelings of loss of control can be a good thing. Many people improve their lives because of it. "They find new ways of being and new meaning in their life," Raymer says.

I allow my desire for control over things in my life to be too important. Once again, I must learn to let go....

My dad says that his diagnostic and surgical hospitalizations left him feeling helpless and totally dependent. "It's a feeling I don't like to have," he says. "I take pride in my independence." He says that he was down, both emotionally and physically, and that the prospect of it going on indefinitely loomed before him. Nevertheless, he viewed his loss of independence and control as an opportunity—a chance for him either to trust or not trust God by faith. "At that very lowest moment, I saw my two choices: to either panic, be afraid, and rely on myself, or to place myself in God's hands and let Him be in control of my situation," he says.

Although my mom's inability to control many aspects in her life was a serious struggle for her, she did several things to combat the dizzying effects of losing control in her life. After doing extensive research and discussing things with her physicians, she made her own medical decisions. She prayed. She read the Bible. She talked with others about what she was going through. She was thankful for past and present blessings. She reached out to those in need. But, most importantly, she really tried to trust God despite dim circumstances.

I must simply cling to the trust I have in the Lord. He will take care of my family. It has been a very good year.

SO, WHO IS GOD, ANYWAY?

While we cannot know everything fully and completely about God, the Bible gives us many details about His character that can comfort us in our staggering circumstances and increase our ability to trust Him.

Max Anders says that God is "an infinite, eternal spirit, creator of the universe and sovereign over it."[1] This is an accurate definition based on the Bible, the Christian's standard of truth. As Christians, we can acknowledge God's sovereignty in our lives because we have biblical assurance that God is God, Lord of heaven and earth. If God is sovereign, He is in complete control of our individual lives as well as everything that goes on around us. He is the captain of our ship, and He alone is in control of our voyage—past, present, and future. Simply put, God is in control.

Strange how one can look back and see how things have worked according to some wonderful plan—but look for-

ward and it is all unchartered ground—a complete mystery. Someday I will look back on tomorrow and know that the right decisions were made and everything fitted wonderfully into the Lord's plans.

We also know that God knows everything and that He can do anything and everything He wants to do. King David penned this beautiful description of God's omniscience and omnipotence:

> O LORD, Thou hast searched me and known me....
> Thou dost scrutinize my path and my lying down,
> And art intimately acquainted with all my ways....
> Thine eyes have seen my unformed substance;
> And in Thy book they were all written,
> The days that were ordained for me,
> When as yet there was not one of them.

PSALM 139:1, 3, 16

Imagine: God knew each one of us before we were even born! No one else knows us as transparently as He does. He even knows how many hairs are on our head (Luke 12:7).

God not only knows all about us, but He also cares about us. The Bible tells us that God is love (1 John 4:8). He values us in a personal way, and He desires what is best for us. God gave us His greatest demonstration of love two thousand years ago, when He sent His only Son, Jesus Christ, to become a man, suffer and die for our sins, and become alive again, so that we might enjoy an eternal relationship with God in heaven. If He loved us that much, we must conclude that He will take care of us in the midst of whatever physical, emotional, and spiritual struggles He allows us to experience. His shepherding provides us with the means to endure life's difficulties.

Understanding God's character gives us a better picture of who He is and how He operates. He is not an unconcerned bystander, powerless to rule over the events, people, and circumstances in our lives. His inherent qualities show that He is someone worthy of our trust as we face life's difficulties. We can safely relinquish control and place our lives in His hands. Believing that God is sovereign, loving, powerful, and good is the foundation for learning how to trust Him, even in the midst of our confusion, anger, doubt, bitterness, and suffering.

One night I was lying awake listening to the sounds of the hospital, suddenly I knew fear as never before. It was a different fear: more an intense awe as the presence of God thrust into my consciousness. He was there with me in all of His magnificence; a holy and incredibly powerful presence. That was it: <u>powerful</u>. He had control of everything in my life. I realized this as never before and it struck a kind of fear, which overwhelmed my senses.

What was I crying about? He had always had control of my life and had sent so much good to me that I began to complain when it appeared that the good was over. He knew that too much good is not healthy for a person for they begin to think that they are doing things right and deserved the good they received so graciously given by the hand of God. In that one moment, I recognized that God loved me and was sending the most powerful message of love to me as I suffered through the most difficult time of my life.

And even this illness could be a blessing. Through it He would lead me to greater understanding of His love and the purpose for which He had called me. I could *accept His challenge or I could slowly die in my self-pity. The choice was clear and I chose to walk with Him. Hope had been born and provided the basis for the beginning of a positive attitude.*

If nothing happens to us without God's knowledge and permission, it follows that God knows and allows some of us to battle physical diseases. But how we choose to respond to this paradox is still very much our own decision.

ARE MIRACLES POSSIBLE?

After attending her afternoon graduate class, Ena Bromley came back to the apartment, her head pounding. A few hours later her headache had grown worse, so she lay down and fell asleep. Three days later she woke up from a coma and discovered that she could no longer walk.

"The doctors told me that I had a fifty-fifty chance of ever walking again," says Ena, who had been diagnosed with dystonia, a neurological movement disorder, two years earlier. Yet one year later Ena could walk without aid. She believes that God performed a miracle. "This miracle is totally undeserved and is completely about God's grace," she says. "I didn't realize what my purpose in life was before this happened to me, and now I do. What I am striving for is what God's will is for my life and not my own goals and success."

What is a *miracle*? According to Webster's dictionary, it is "an extraordinary event manifesting divine intervention in human affairs." This definition presupposes a belief in a closed universe in which God has the ability, power, and right to intervene at any time.

"God is sovereign and omniscient and can accomplish what He wants, whenever He wants," says Rev. Mark Tindle. He adds that although the Bible clearly supports the existence of miracles, we cannot predict where, when, how, or why they occur. "I think it's safe to say that God's miracles are ultimately meant to bring glory to

Himself—it's certainly not a magic show or healing tent," Tindle says. "There are purposes that transcend our lives, our crises, and our prayers." The danger lies in aligning your prayers with physical healing rather than with God and His will. Praying for a miracle is not the same as demanding one.[2]

Dr. Christie Hunley has observed families dealing with a terminally ill child in two very different ways. In one case, church friends came to the hospital to pray for the child. Unfortunately, these visitors encouraged the family to pray in a way that allowed for only one outcome—that God would miraculously heal him. "These well-meaning people really interfered with the family accepting this child's impending death, which was extremely obvious," Hunley says. "It really deprived them of the last time they were going to have meaningful time together. This whole situation was disturbing to me and seemed to cause great distress to the family. It is not that I believe God couldn't do something, but it realistically didn't seem like He was going to."

Hunley recalls how another family in similar circumstances handled the situation. "This family talked to their child, explained the possibility of death, and told him he would go to heaven. It was very peaceful because they were so accepting of what was happening. I could really see God helping them through all of it."[3]

According to Bill Hill, a retired pastor and chaplain who is battling cancer, the greater miracle is that God's grace is sufficient for us to continue on in the face of great difficulties. "A group of deacons from my church came here, laid hands on me, and prayed for my healing," Hill says. "It was a powerful experience, and I really felt it; but I was concerned about their discouragement if God chose not to heal me." Based on God's promise, Hill is confident that he will have enough grace to handle whatever happens.

How should one approach prayer for healing? In *Why Do People Suffer?* James Jones says that Christians should not try to command or manipulate the power of God, however worthy the cause.

"Instead, they are called to submit to the sovereign power of God who answers prayers as He decides. His will is supreme.... To the Christian who follows Jesus through death into heaven, dying is seen as the ultimate healing. That is why to pray to God for healing from a terminal disease and not to be healed physically is as much an answer to prayer as to be given more life on earth."[4]

Miracles are possible, but God dictates their application. Tindle suggests that when we pray for a miracle, we should base our prayers on what we know about God's compassionate nature and acknowledge that we are dependent upon His healing power. "Part of how I pray for miracles is that people will look and see how incredible God truly is, but I also pray that the needs for strength, comfort, and peace will be met."

TRUSTING GOD IN SPITE OF YOURSELF

When I was eight or nine years old, my parents played a game with my sister and me in order to help us learn what trust felt like. While we waited upstairs, they moved chairs, couches, and tables out of their ordinary spots and created a maze in the family room. Then they put blindfolds on us and told us to listen carefully to their instructions.

"Take three steps to your left," my mom commanded. "Stop. Go two steps forward." At first it felt awkward to take one step after another in darkness, but gradually we became more comfortable relying on our parents for direction.

"Now, I want you to fall backwards," Mom said.

My muscles immediately tensed up as I stood there, unwilling to obey. Her voice was unmistakably in front of me. *How can she catch me if she isn't behind me?* I thought. I literally refused to do it. Rebecca, on the other hand, had no qualms about letting go of her fears and free falling into the air—right into the arms of my father, who was standing behind her ready to catch her.

Why couldn't I do it that first time? Even though I loved my parents and thought I trusted them, something held me back. I didn't have complete faith that they would catch me because from what I knew about where they were standing, it seemed impossible.

As I grew in my Christian walk during high school and college, I thought that I really loved God and trusted Him completely. It wasn't until my mom was diagnosed with cancer that I realized that I trusted Him only as long as everything was going fine.

Tindle says that an illness brings to the forefront our natural desire to control our own lives. "Our comfort zones have been shattered," he says, "and these difficult situations will most likely cause a clash between self-centeredness and God's way." My reaction to my mom's illness was a daily, if not moment-by-moment, struggle with distrust. The situation seemed bigger than God's caring arms, and unless I submitted myself to God and asked for His help, my response was usually one of extreme sadness, anger, and anxiety.

It has taken me a long time to give up trying to control my life and allow God to show me where I should go and what I should do each moment of every day. This is much easier said than done, and it is a process that never ends. When life's supports are stripped from us, our natural instinct is to grip the steering wheel as hard as we can and not permit God even to sit in the front seat with us, much less drive. How do I know when I am trying to control my own life? I notice that I start directing everyone around me so that they will think and do things my way. When a wrench is thrown into my plans, I tend to become upset, anxious, and frustrated.

How do you react when your plans go awry?

In order to experience God's peace, comfort, and joy, it is not enough to merely acknowledge God's sovereignty and love. We must trust Him with everything in our lives and let Him be in control.

Attitudes and actions together define the level of our ability to trust God. This ability impacts what we do in life, as well as how we feel emotionally and, sometimes, physically. If trust is an ongoing struggle and never totally finished, how do we recognize it? How do we really trust God and let Him have control? Trust has several components. Here, they are listed separately, but keep in mind that this is not a step-by-step formula.

Confession

One night when my mom was in the hospital undergoing treatment, sleep eluded me. I had become so anxious and worried that my stomach hurt, and I literally felt nauseous. I read through Psalms and Proverbs, clinging to their promises. As I did, I noticed the correlation between comfort and trust. "He is a shield to those who take refuge in Him" (Proverbs 30:5). "Those who trust in the Lord are as mount Zion, which cannot be moved, but abides forever" (Psalm 125:1).

Then I looked up Jeremiah 17:5. "Thus says the Lord, 'Cursed is the man who trusts in mankind and makes flesh his strength, and whose heart turns away from the Lord.'" The sinfulness of worry glared at me. This verse summed up exactly why I usually worry. I tend to turn away from God and rely on myself until my power is gone. I have to consciously be aware of this sinful inclination and ask God's forgiveness whenever I succumb to it.

It is imperative to confess the sin of worry because it means you are not trusting God. Jesus told His disciples, "Do not be anxious for your life"; and He reminded them that God cared for them more than for the ravens, lilies, and field grass (Luke 12:22–34). Have you ever viewed your worry or lack of trust in God as a sin? Stop now and ask God to forgive you for worrying about_____

_____.

Praise

"Let everything that has breath praise the Lord. Praise the Lord!" The last verse of the book of Psalms calls attention to the importance of praise in our lives. I must admit that when my mom was sick and dying, praising God was the last thing I felt like doing. *How in the world can I praise or thank God for her cancer?* I asked myself.

However, what I witnessed over and over again was how God took care of her, gave her strength, comforted her, and filled her with His peace when she needed it the most. Instead of praising God for the cancer and the side effects of chemotherapy, I began to praise Him for His faithfulness and constant shepherding. Concentrating on God's character allowed me to be filled with praise instead of anger, bitterness, or worry.

> *Praise Him! For every step of the way He has been guiding me. I have had difficulty in these last two and a half weeks to get out of myself because I have not felt so well. This has been a difficult treatment. My spirit has been silenced, and I feel sort of in a hole—but it will soar again. Once again, I shall rejoice. I have been given the gift of life and the secret of life.*

Daniel R. Mitchum says:

Seeking first the Kingdom of God means worshipping the Lord of hosts, the Creator of the universe. It is praising Him for who He is and not merely for what He does. As we become people who can praise the Lord in spite of our needs, He has promised that we will become a people who will find their needs met.[5]

Are you willing to praise God for who He is? It will take practice because cultivating a heart of praise does not happen overnight. For starters, think about the attributes of God's character that have special meaning in your life right now. Begin by praising God for _____. At the very minimum, praise God once a day.

Tonight I am alone. It is a good time to talk with the Lord. I praise Him! Little by little I am learning to delight in His presence and to praise Him for who He is, not for what He does. I have such little imagination. I find it hard to understand anything that isn't a concrete example. It is necessary for the Lord to call me back from time to time because I tend so easily to assume things about my life that I should not.

Acceptance

When I was in high school, I usually felt comfortable at home and at church, but not at school or other public places. I attributed my shyness and resistance to participating in activities to being introverted.

During the summer before my sophomore year in high school, I started a three-year, Camper-in-Leadership training program at a Pioneer Girls camp in east Texas. This rigorous program forced me to do things that I would never have chosen to do on my own—like praying in front of a hundred people and leading a songfest for the entire camp at dinnertime. For two weeks I was tied up in knots, chiding myself whenever I didn't do something perfectly. I felt unworthy and extremely unhappy with myself.

Talking with my camp counselor one evening, I told her how I felt. I'll never forget what she said. "Do you know that when you put yourself down, you're putting God down? He made you, and God doesn't make junk." Then she asked me, "How does God see you in light of your acceptance of Jesus Christ as your Savior?" Reading from Ephesians, I discovered, "For he chose us in him before the creation of the world to be holy and blameless in his sight" (Ephesians 1:4, NIV). That evening marked a major turning point in my life. I realized that I cannot base my acceptance of myself on what I think or feel, or even on how I perform or behave.

Viewing yourself as God does is crucial when a physical illness changes or destroys something from which you previously gained self-esteem. Remember that even though you have changed, God has not. He still loves and accepts you exactly as before.

First, I have to reevaluate the basis of my self-image. Immediately three things come to mind: (1) strength—I was proud of my strength; physical and emotional. I could gut anything out, especially physically; (2) health—I had always eaten right and was proud of being so healthy. There were times when I looked down on others weaker than I; (3) self-sufficiency—I didn't need to depend on anyone else for anything. I could work things out myself. I could learn to do most anything from financial to mechanical. This disease does not allow me to retain these false securities. I now need to depend on others for my strength, my health, and things that have to get done. Most of all I need to learn to depend on God for my life.

How would you rate your self-esteem? Do you accept and love yourself the way Jesus loves and accepts you? If not, what one thing stands in the way? Write down the one thing you cannot love about yourself: _____. What do you think God would say about this one thing? Would God be unable to love or accept you because of it? Can you base your acceptance of yourself on God's perspective of you rather than on your estimation or that of someone else?

By the same token, have you come to a place of acceptance about your particular situation? Identify one aspect of your situation that you are having a difficult time accepting: _____
_____.

Bring this before God in prayer and leave it at His feet. No matter how insurmountable your situation may seem, God has the power to help you adapt and endure.

Gratitude and Remembrance

Whenever I have a hard time believing that God will take care of me in a crisis, I take time to look back over my life and recount all of the things He has already done for me. Throughout my mom's illness, I purposely tried to find things for which I could thank God. Oftentimes they would help me remember that God loves and cares about me.

I was newly married when my mom was diagnosed with cancer. My pregnancy with our first son, Joshua, was unplanned and seemed to come at a difficult time for us, financially and professionally. Yet I soon realized that Joshua had been far from unplanned; he had entered our lives at the perfect moment. We moved to Maryland just prior to his birth and bought a house only minutes away from my parents' home. My mom's full year of remission coincided with the first year of Joshua's life, and she basked in the delight of grandmotherhood.

What are you thankful for? How do you think God has blessed you over your lifetime? Try writing out a list of everything you believe God has blessed you with in the past. Make it as long as you can, and keep it where you can look at it again and again.

Obedience and Laying Aside Self

Think back to your early childhood, and try to remember why Mr. McGregor almost caught Peter Rabbit in his garden. "'Now, my dears,' said old Mrs. Rabbit one morning, 'you may go into the fields or down the lane, but don't go into Mr. McGregor's garden. Your father had an accident there, and Mrs. McGregor put him in a pie.'" Peter didn't obey his mother's instructions. If he had, he would have enjoyed bread, milk, and blackberries for supper that night along with his siblings.

Obedience is one important way we can put our trust in God into action. God knows what is best for us and, for the most part, lays it out clearly in the Bible. We become more obedient when we put aside our own will and desires and follow His lead. The apostle Paul urges us to lay aside the old self so that we can be renewed in the spirit of our minds and conformed to God's image (Ephesians 4:21–24).

It began to come through what the Lord is trying to teach me. I can become upset at these situations, or I can decide that I am really worthless anyway, or I can accept it as part of dying to self. If I truly believe that only the Lord can make my life worthwhile, then I must allow Him to control all aspects of my life—including the waiting. He alone can redeem that time. The two to three days I am in the hospital are all waits.

This inner transformation of laying aside self has to happen over and over again in our lives. We have an ongoing choice, every day and every moment of our lives, either to be sensitive to what God wants for us, or to do whatever we feel like doing.

I enjoy a wonderfully deep friendship and loving relationship with my husband, and I thank God for having blessed me with him. However, there are times when we argue and say hurtful things to each other. God has been working on me over the years to bend my selfish and proud will. How hard it is for me to ask my husband for his forgiveness! I certainly do not feel like doing it, yet I know that is what God wants me to do. Many times I plead for God to help me say those words because they just don't want to come out of my mouth. Forgiveness and reconciliation are choices I need to make regularly in my marriage if I want it to remain strong and healthy.

Similarly, when we face tough circumstances, we need to be especially aware of what God wants us to do in our situation and obey Him without fail. "It is the easiest thing in the world to obey God when he commands us to do what we like and to trust Him when the path is all sunshine," said Theodore L. Cuyler, a nineteenth-century Presbyterian clergyman. "The real victory of faith is to trust God in the dark and through the dark."

In which areas in your life are you being obedient to God? Which areas show disobedience? Are you ready to ask God where He wants you to be and what He wants you to be doing? Spend some time in prayer to ask God where He might be leading you.

When the Lord commands obedience, I have no other option. I am His; He has asked me to suffer; I will obey and do it with rejoicing.

"Even if you can no longer direct how you live physically, you can always maintain power over how you live psychologically," observes Irene Pollin.[6] Her observation is particularly meaningful to people who recognize God as the ultimate source of power. Through God's grace and power, we can learn to relinquish control to Him and be at peace with our life circumstances. God has promised to give us a peace that surpasses all of our human understanding (Philippians 4:6, 7). As you cling to that promise, you will be better able to deal with the "why" questions that frequently accompany the diagnosis of a life-threatening illness.

F

TOOLS FOR OVERCOMING THE SENSATION OF LOSS OF CONTROL

Using practical coping methods can help reduce or minimize some of the emotional and psychosocial effects of losing control. If you're ready to take some additional steps toward peace of mind, grab a pen or pencil and spend some time working through the following exercises.[7]

Make Your Own Decisions

Making decisions, large or small, can help you feel in charge. You may want to start with small decisions and build up to bigger ones. In the area of your medical treatment and procedures, asserting your decision-making powers can be one of the best ways of exercising control. You can do in-depth research, seek advice, talk to your spouse or trusted friend, get a second opinion, and try to be responsible for as many decisions as you can.

List five situations where you could take the initiative in decision-making in the next two to three weeks. (Do not forget "little" things such as what you wear, what you eat or drink, where you sleep, and what music you listen to.)

1._____

2._____

3._____

4._____

5._____

Separate Long-Term Problems from Immediate Ones

Take a few minutes to write down all of the problems you think you are facing right now (use the extra page at the end of this chapter if you need more room). Next to it, write either *long* for long-term problem or *short* for short-term problem. Then jot down possible solutions for each problem. (You may want to enlist a close friend or family member to brainstorm with you.) Finally, put the problems in the order you want to deal with them. This method can be very effective, especially for those people who enjoy organization, to-do lists, and the like.

PROBLEM	LONG OR SHORT	SOLUTIONS/CHOICES

1._____

_____

2._____

_____

3._____

_____

4._____

_____

5._____

_____

Plan Ahead, but Be Flexible and Creative

By anticipating and minimizing surprises, you can stay in better control of situations. Adding more structure to your life can give you a sense of mastery and control. Tightening and planning your weekly or daily schedule is one good way to do that. However, because no one can predict future events with certainty, try to be as flexible and creative in your life as you can.

To implement the first part of this coping method, you need to make a sample schedule of the weekly activities and responsibilities with which you need help. Be as specific and detailed as possible. For example, if you have a doctor's appointment, based on your past experiences, plan enough time to get there, wait in the office, go through any billing paperwork, and return home.

Sunday

_____

_____

Monday

_____

_____

Tuesday

_____

_____

Wednesday

_____

_____

Thursday

_____

_____

FRIDAY

_____

_____

SATURDAY

_____

_____

Next, look over your weekly schedule and pick several things that could throw you an unexpected curveball. For example, a doctor's visit might take up more time than you anticipated. What does this mean for the rest of your day? Maybe the person who plans to drive you needs to be somewhere else soon after the appointment. Consider creating a backup plan in case he has to leave before you are ready.

Another example of planning ahead might be to decide beforehand what you might do or say if a surprise visitor arrives at an inopportune moment. If you are prepared, you will feel more in control of the situation. What are some other surprises you could anticipate and plan for ahead of time?

If planning for the future is important to you and you feel that it would not cause you anxiety at this point, write down five things you would like to help plan. For instance, you could help your children pick out colleges that they might want to consider attending; you could design a family getaway weekend (if you cannot leave home, then have fun selecting activities or events that could be done in your own house); you could research the possibilities of taking a class or learning a new hobby (some colleges now offer courses via the Internet, or a hobby enthusiast might be willing to come to your home for demonstrations); or you could take a serious look at your finances and make necessary adjustments for any potential life changes.

Plans to Consider

1._____

2._____

3._____

4._____

5._____

Evaluate Whom You Can Count On

Think about which people you can comfortably rely on for support. Seek out those who will just let you talk and not tell you what you should do or think or feel. This coping method is designed to help you feel more confident in the resources you have available. Maybe you don't even realize how much support you already have. If this is an area that discourages you or makes you fearful, consider the possibility that some people in your life may not know where or how they can help you and are just waiting for you to ask.

Try to write down the names of at least ten people and what you can comfortably expect or accept from them. You may want to include reasons why you can trust and depend on them. If there's a question about what you expect from a particular individual, it's a good idea to talk with him and get his assent.

Individual's Name	What He Can Do	Why You Trust Him

1._____

_____

2._____

_____

3._____

_____

4._____

_____

5._____

_____

6._____

_____

7._____

_____

8._____

_____

9._____

_____

10._____

_____

Join a Support Group

Not feeling alone in your physical, emotional, and spiritual struggles can be very comforting. If you desire, search out support groups through community, health, hospital and/or church organizations. Keep in mind that there are groups for individuals as well as families.

Visit at least two support-group meetings, or try meeting individually or as a family with a social worker, psychologist, counselor, or spiritual advisor who has experience working with the seriously ill and their families. You can get referrals or recommendations from your local hospital, hospice organization, church, or national organizations such as the National Hospice and Palliative Care Organization (NHPCO), the American Cancer Society, and the National Institutes of Health.

Group or individual visited_____
Contact/telephone number_____
My response/thoughts_____

Group or individual visited_____
Contact/telephone number_____
My response/thoughts_____

Group or individual visited_____
Contact/telephone number_____
My response/thoughts_____

Group or individual visited_____
Contact/telephone number_____
My response/thoughts_____

Be Involved in the Lives of Others

Having a heart for others keeps self-pity at bay. While you may not be physically able to do as much as you would like, you can carry out the important task of praying for those in need. If you are up to it, call or write notes of encouragement to others. Who around you needs encouragement?

Think of at least one person you could encourage either through prayer or through written or verbal means. Write down several specific ways you could encourage him. Practice doing this as often as you can.

"I loathe my own life; I will give full vent to my complaint;
I will speak in the bitterness of my soul.
I will say to God, 'Do not condemn me;
Let me know why Thou dost contend with me.
Is it right for Thee indeed to oppress, to reject the labor of Thy hands,
And to look favorably on the schemes of the wicked?
Hast Thou eyes of flesh?
Or dost Thou see as a man sees?
Are Thy days as the days of a mortal,
Or Thy years as man's years,
That Thou shouldst seek for my guilt, and search after my sin?
According to Thy knowledge I am indeed not guilty;
Yet there is no deliverance from Thy hand...
Didst Thou not pour me out like milk,
And curdle me like cheese;
Clothe me with skin and flesh,
And knit me together with bones and sinews?
Thou hast granted me life and lovingkindness;
And Thy care has preserved my spirit.
Yet these things Thou hast concealed in Thy heart;
I know that this is within Thee.'"

JOB 10:1–7, 10–13

F
Severe trouble in a believer has the effect of
loosening the roots of his soul earthward and
tightening the anchor-hold of his heart heavenward.

CHARLES HADDON SPURGEON

THREE

If I Am
Indeed His

M om, why is metal hard? Why is it cold in space? Why do I have to do homework? Why doesn't that person have a place to sleep at night? Why can't that little boy walk?"

"Why" questions have been a daily part of my life since my children started talking. I answer my sons' questions seriously because I realize that they are figuring out their world and how they fit into it. Some of their questions are easy to answer; others are difficult and require me to do a little research. Some of their questions have answers that make sense only to adults; still others do not really have answers. Adults also ask questions about things that bother them. "Why didn't I get that job? Why does my husband ignore my feelings? Why doesn't my body look like _____?" Eventually, both children and adults find answers that make sense, or they decide that certain questions are unanswerable.

When catastrophe strikes, however, most people find themselves trying to make sense of their lives by questioning everything anew. If you are reevaluating your life through a lens that has magnified suffering, you and your family may find yourselves trying to give meaning to your illness by searching for the reason for it. This chapter looks at several common emotional and spiritual reactions to serious illness in the context of biblical truths about the realities of life.

Life Is Not Fair

Marjory L. Purvis will never forget December 26, 1978—the day her thirty-year-old daughter, Janey, was diagnosed with terminal breast cancer. Janey, who was pregnant with her third child, had been told that a lump in her breast was just an enlarged milk gland, but seven months into her pregnancy the lump grew rapidly and metastasized. She began radiation treatments immediately, and on January 16, 1979, doctors performed a cesarean section, delivered a baby boy eight weeks prematurely, and told Janey that she had no more than six months to live.

"Life isn't supposed to go this way!" Marjory says. "Somewhere it is 'written' that the elderly are to die first—like old cars or lawn mowers—and we accept that with sadness, of course. But to have one's dear, beautiful daughter sentenced to die—surely, it's a mistake."

Marjory couldn't understand *why* her daughter was dying. Janey did not smoke or drink, and she was a "good Christian mother." "Somehow I believed that those things should have protected her from something this horrible," Marjory says.

Suddenly, life takes on new meaning. As a Christian, I thought I had worked through my beliefs of life and death and was confident that I was living as I should. I was active in my church and when there was a moral choice to be made, I chose to be honest, chaste, and truthful. In fact, I chaffed at the way the world had deteriorated. There was no longer a standard of living, which I considered crucial if one is to follow the commandments set forth in Scripture.

Not only did I follow the rules, but I also knew

that I was Jesus' own. I had accepted Him 25 years earlier. I trusted Him for all things in my life, diligently trying to walk with Him through prayer and Bible reading. For some reason, I fully believed He would protect me from some of the worst things in life—cancer was one of those things. And so when I was found to have cancer, I felt betrayed. "Lord, this was not part of the bargain! How can I serve You if I am dying of cancer?"

His answer was not immediately comforting. "I am with you," He said. I had wanted to hear, "I will cure you."

To emphasize the point of no cure, medical professionals come to me to inform me of my choices for further treatment. One thing they all point out is that no matter what I choose, there are no promises. Even if I go through their most horrible treatments, I have no assurance that they will work.

Why? is an inevitable question. When you struggle to understand the reasons for and timing of a health crisis, the natural psychological response is to conclude that everything you are facing—pain, suffering, fear, and changed circumstances—is unfair. "Most people experience this feeling," says Daniel Haffey, "and there's real truth to the unfairness of life because it's the result of a sinful world with sinful people." What we really want is not what's fair, he adds, but what we think is best for us.

Mark Tindle agrees that life is not fair no matter how *fair* is defined, but he also points out that the unfairness of life is due to the fact that we are part of a fallen creation in a fallen world. "We tend to look at our external surroundings, such as relationships, financial security, education, physical prowess, social success, and assume that that is the sum total of life."

How can you handle the feeling that life is not fair?

As a patient, you can:

- Allow yourself to feel this feeling.
- "Yell" at God if necessary. (Be wary of getting stuck in this mode, however.)
- Express your feelings in a journal.
- Talk with a friend or family member about your feelings.
- Try to accept that life *is* unfair because it does involve pain and loss.
- Find one small thing you are grateful for despite your circumstances.
- Realize that although no one is immune to trouble in this world, Jesus has already conquered the world (John 16:33).
- Rest in God's promises of peace and comfort. He will never forsake you!

As a family member or friend, you can:

- Avoid clichés like "Well, it must be God's will for you" or "You just need to trust God more."
- Acknowledge and empathize with your loved one's feelings of unfairness without supporting unrealistic expectations.
- Remember that your loved one may not really be looking for answers to questions about life's fairness; he may just want you to listen.
- Demonstrate through your presence that you care for your loved one.
- Pray for and with your loved one.
- Offer words of encouragement, love, support, and acceptance.

Remember also that God will provide you with peace and comfort as you face your "unfair" illness. Here are some of His promises to those who lean on and trust Him:

- God will restore your soul (Psalm 23:3).

- God will guide you and lead you in the path of righteousness (Psalm 23:3; 25:9–10).

- God is your help and your shield (Psalm 33:20).

- God will sustain you (Psalm 55:22).

- God will empathize with you better than the closest friend because He had to endure suffering, too (Isaiah 53; Hebrews 2:9, 18; 4:14–16).

- God will give you a future and plan and a hope (Jeremiah 29:11).

- God will comfort you (Matthew 5:4; 2 Corinthians 1:3–5; 7:6).

- God will never leave or forsake you (Matthew 28:20).

- God Himself will intercede for you (Romans 8:26–27).

- God will never allow anything to separate you from His love (Romans 8:35–39).

- God will give you victory—perhaps here on earth, but certainly in eternity with Him (Romans 8:37).

- God has prepared a place in heaven for you (1 Corinthians 2:9).

- God will give you peace that surpasses all human comprehension (Philippians 4:6–7).

- God will give you the grace and strength to do whatever becomes necessary to endure (Philippians 4:13; Hebrews 4:16).

- God has power over death (Revelation 1:17–18).

- Ultimately, God will wipe away every tear (Revelation 7:16–17; 21:4), and He will destroy death and Hades (Revelation 20:14).

Which of these promises brings you the most comfort, hope, and encouragement as you face serious illness? You might want to memorize them so that you can offer the same comfort to others.

I've Done Something Wrong

One of the biggest hurdles you may need to clear is a nagging feeling that your illness is a kind of punishment. David Watson was an English clergyman who died of cancer at age fifty. In *Fear No Evil*, he described his tendency to see his illness as punishment for sin—until he was reminded of God's love:

> Sometimes I have thought of my asthma or cancer as being punishment for sin. I remember with shame many foolish things I have done in the past, and with a fairly sensitive conscience it is not hard to feel both guilty and condemned. I am thoroughly aware of my failings and only too willing to believe that my sickness is what I deserve—indeed much less than I deserve. As far as straight justice is concerned that is true. But when I reflect on God's love and mercy in the scriptures I am comforted, especially when that love is *shown* by other Christians around me.[1]

Job also questioned whether his illness and calamities were due to his sin: "Have I sinned? What have I done to Thee, O watcher of men? Why hast Thou set me as Thy target, so that I am a burden to myself?" (Job 7:20). Philip Yancey says that the book of Job disproves the idea that every time we suffer, God is punishing us or trying to tell us something specific. "Sometimes God does send suffering as a punishment (as in the ten plagues of Egypt), *but you cannot argue backwards,* as Job's friends tried to do, and assume that each incident of suffering can be linked to a specific failure."[2]

Tindle says that every sin committed cannot be linked to direct punishment from God because the Crucifixion was God's punishment for sins. He is careful to point out that this whole issue is tricky because we cannot say that God never punishes His people. But we do know that if God does punish, it is for a loving purpose and not a vengeful thing (see Proverbs 3:11, 12 and Hebrews 12:5–11). God's discipline can be compared to a parent disciplining a child. The purpose is not to get back at the child for his behavior, but to teach and model a better way to act or respond. God also disciplines us for our good so that we may share His holiness (Hebrews 12:10).

> I immediately have had a hard time accepting the sentence, which has been imposed on me. I guess I bought into the message that the Lord would bless those who followed Him faithfully and if you become ill or poor, that means your faith somehow does not measure up. I have always argued that this was not biblical, yet now when faced with my own trials, it is quite natural to assume that I somehow failed in my walk with the Lord. I feel like I am being punished.
>
> It is easy enough to feel punished when you know that there are lots of things which are not quite right in your attitudes. I know that I deserve it. Yet, as I look around me, I also know that I am not the only one who should be punished if that is the way it works....
>
> There is a comfort to know that God is in control. It certainly is better than having only the doctors in control for they do not seem sure about how things are going

to work out, and I most definitely do not want Satan to be in control.

At this same time, I realize how final death is and that I really am not sure what I will meet on that other side. I have always had a hard time feeling assured that my commitment to the Lord is what it should be and at this time I wonder if I am indeed His. Part of this concern comes from an ingrained idea that the Lord would not allow such a horrible thing to happen to one of His children. I feel like I am being punished and had I just been a better Christian, this would not have happened to me. I really am sure that people would look at me and see that I have not been good enough and God is judging me. I am ashamed and embarrassed.

Well-meaning friends and family members need to be careful not to suggest that their loved one's illness is due to a specific sin in his life. Even if bad choices contributed to the illness, do not infer (even casually) that if the patient changed a behavior or attitude, God would heal him. Instead, stress God's—and your own—unconditional love and acceptance.

I have not sought the Lord as I should have and now feel alone. But, I know He is with me. I always feel guilty at these times—like I have brought the recurrence [of cancer] upon myself by not abiding in Christ as I should have. Such thoughts, though, are unworthy and make Him into a hard taskmaster. So, this cannot be true.

Eugene Clark had been working as a composer and organist for Back to the Bible Broadcast in Lincoln, Nebraska, when the medication he was taking for his arthritis ate holes in his stomach, causing two life-threatening hemorrhages. He had to discontinue use of the medication, and arthritis took over his entire body. Within a few weeks, the thirty-eight-year-old was bedridden and blind.

For nineteen years Eugene lay in bed, blind and crippled with arthritis, yet he continued to compose and arrange music. During that time, friends and strangers alike sent him letters or visited him at home to tell him what they felt the Lord had revealed to them about why he was sick.

One woman was totally against making any changes in a musical score. "It is a sin against the composer and against God for anyone to tamper with a musical composition," she told Eugene. "That is the reason you are lying there blind and helpless. God is punishing you for what you are doing. If you will confess your sin and stop doing this dastardly thing, He will restore your health."[3]

How do you think Eugene felt after that woman's visit? Fortunately, he was able to listen politely to her and state his own convictions. But can you imagine being told that? How would that kind of visitor make you feel?

In *Hope for the Troubled Heart,* Billy Graham says:

> It is unkind to attribute every accident, every illness and sorrow to God's punishment for wrong behavior. It is appalling how many Christians approach suffering friends with that principle. They visit first with words of comfort, and then leave a load of guilt behind ("What could you have done to deserve this?") or pious advice ("Perhaps you need to pray harder").[4]

Right now it may be difficult for you to feel God's love and concern. The real question is not whether God is punishing you for your sins, but whether you believe that God loves you and wants the best for you. God loved us while we were still unrepentant sinners, and He continues to love us, no matter what—even though we might not *feel* His love.

How can you wrestle with the feeling that you have done something wrong?

As a patient, you can:

- Remind yourself that God is not vindictive.
- Focus on your present relationship with God, not on what was in the past.
- Realize that, even though you may be reaping the consequences of bad choices you made in the past, God loves you no matter what.
- Memorize God's comforting words to you in the Bible.
- Listen to praise and worship music.

As a friend or family member, you can:

- Allow your loved one to ask, "Am I to blame?" Remember that questioning is normal and can be healing.
- Let your loved one talk his way through this feeling. Do not hurry him.
- Defend God's character on this issue very carefully. Point out that God is not vindictive.
- Never say, "Confess your sin(s), and then God will heal you."

GOD IS TO BLAME

When a young man's wife was diagnosed with cancer, he told her, "If you die, I'll never have anything to do with God again." He blamed God for her illness, and he was angry—very angry. You might be feeling angry right now, too. Oftentimes, God becomes the target of anger when people believe that He could have influenced the outcome of a certain situation but didn't. *Why didn't He?* they ask.

Haffey says that anger is a reaction to feelings of loss of control and pain and that it's an important stage in accepting a loss. "None of us like it when other people are angry, so the biggest challenge is tolerating their anger," says Haffey. "We need to validate their anger and remember that it comes from pain, but we also need to avoid getting caught up in it." Most people eventually realize that being angry isn't going to make a difference.

I must admit that I was extremely angry with God for several months after my mom was diagnosed and then again after her death. I felt as if God had dealt my family and me an unfair hand in life. Because I believed that God was all-powerful and all-good, I was confused, hurt, and upset that He hadn't intervened in my mom's illness; and I concluded that He was ultimately to blame for it.

In my bouts with anger, I discovered that its tight grip lessened with each passing week until finally it flared up in occasional bursts of emotion. I allowed myself to be angry, but I knew deep down that I did not want to stay angry forever. At first when I prayed, I simply told God that I was really angry with Him. Sometimes no words came because I was crying too hard. *Why, God? Why did You do this? I'm so mad. This is terrible. I cannot bear it.* Then, slowly, my prayers softened to whispers of acceptance: *You know that I do not like this one bit and that my heart feels like it is breaking. Help my lack of understanding. Give me strength. Help me.*

How can you work through the feeling that God is to blame?

As a patient, you can:
- Allow yourself to be angry.
- Talk to a close friend, family member, pastor, social worker, or psychologist about your anger.
- Pray about your anger—be honest with God.
- Decide when enough anger is enough.

As a friend or family member, you can:
- Allow your loved one to be angry. Don't foster it, but don't squelch it, either.

- Listen, listen, and listen some more.
- Be silent. Don't feel as though you have to give an answer.
- Reinforce God's love, which is best shown flowing through you.
- Lend them your source of comfort—God.

Why Me?

Mounds of pillows lay next to and underneath my mom, who appeared to be sleeping when I peeked into her darkened bedroom.

She turned toward the opened door. "Don't worry," she said. "I'm awake. Come on in."

"I didn't disturb you, did I?" I asked. I knew what a light sleeper she was.

"I'm just resting," she replied. "There's nothing else I can do, right?"

Her question made me realize how trapped she felt. Here I was, about to tell her my plans for the rest of the day, and she couldn't even leave the house. Due to extremely low blood counts during the previous month, she had had to cancel a trip with my dad, lunch with a friend, and call in sick at work three or four times. Of course, she felt disappointed, discouraged, and even envious of others' ability to lead normal lives.

Is there any end to this? Will I ever live a halfway normal life again?

I, too, wished for our family to enjoy a normal life. I observed the lives of my friends and saw that they still had what we had lost: spontaneity, predictability, independence, freedom from treatments, and seeming control of life. I wanted those things back so desperately that I became envious of my friends. I envied them that their moms weren't sick, that they didn't have to worry about losing a parent, that they could run off on a weekend trip without thinking about the "what ifs," and that their lives weren't constantly disrupted and put on hold.

> *Can I ever get free of the sin I continually hold to—that of not accepting my condition? I still fight with wishing I were well and not trusting the Lord that He knows best for me. It is a continual battle—this fight for full trust in the Lord and I feel so weak and tired—especially after a treatment. At this point the enemy has victory and I suffer from if not depression at least a severe sadness—a deep yearning to live as others live. It's hard to believe that I am set apart for something different and to allow the Lord to bring my life into flower.*

Envying a person who has something you don't is a natural, human response. "It is a defensive avoidance of dealing with what is," says Haffey. "But, we cannot stay in this place if we're going to move on." Envy, like anger, is an endless cul-de-sac because the feeling is just not going to help us.

Envy, however, is more than a psychological issue—it's a sin that needs to be confessed immediately. When people get wrapped up with envy, they tend to lose sight of the many things that God has already done (and continues to do) for them. It can be helpful for a loved one to confront an envious person. "It needs to be dealt with on a spiritual level in a relationship or community rather than in isolation," Tindle says.

Bill Hill was originally diagnosed with bladder cancer and is now battling throat and lung cancer. To help reduce his risk of catching a virus or cold, he spent several months at home isolated from crowds and public places. One afternoon a group of friends stopped in for a visit after a round of golf.

"I just couldn't help feeling jealous of them," says Hill. "There they were in healthy bodies, and here I was getting cabin fever and wanting to go golfing, too."

Hill reminded himself that although his friends were going through good times right then, they weren't immune to being sick and having problems. Instead of envying them, he told himself that he should be thankful that they could enjoy whatever time they had. Hill laid his envy to rest with this thought: "Feel good for them like they are feeling sorry for you."

How can you get beyond envying others?

As a patient, you can:

- Stay close to God and ask Him to deepen your relationship.
- Make a list of ten things God has blessed you with since you became ill.
- Remember that even if you are "in tune with God," you can still experience pangs of envy.
- Confront it truthfully.
- Talk about your envy problem with anyone who may unwittingly be making your struggle more difficult.

As a friend or family member, you can:

- Be sensitive to your loved one's feelings.
- Show respect.
- Help your loved one see the good things in his life.
- Realize that at times your loved one may envy you your health and circumstances. Talk about your life only if it is appropriate and you sense that your loved one wants to hear about it.
- Confront in love only after much prayer and consideration, and extend grace and forgiveness when you do.

How Do I Get Past the "Whys"?

There must come a time when you move beyond asking "Why did this happen to me?" to "How am I going to respond?" You, and you alone, are in charge of the decision to accept and adapt to your illness. Some find this easier than others. In many ways, the assimilation process hinges on your relationship with God and your perspective on your health situation. Where does God fit into all of this? How do you think God views your health in His plan for your life?

Rev. Robert E. Steinke says the choice is clear: "Are you ready to live your life with your Christian faith, even if it is a faith that does not have all the answers?" He says that everyone has the choice either to be angry, resentful, embittered, and unhappy in the face of an illness, or to look for a deeper meaning and purpose.[5]

According to Tindle, getting past the "whys" involves getting back to what we believe about God's character and sovereignty. "We need to come to the point where we can say, 'Okay, I don't understand or like this, but I know You are in this with me.'"

The first step is to remember who God really is and what is trustworthy about Him. Search the Scriptures. Read biographies of Christians who have suffered before you. Talk with a pastor, counselor, friend, or family member whose faith you admire and respect. Recount His past blessings and answers to prayer. Pray like you've never prayed before. Ask God to show Himself to you.

Once you have affirmed your belief in God's love and goodness, lay out all your grief, anger, disappointment, worry, fear, and lack of understanding. Lay them before God and at the foot of the cross. Do not hold anything back. Ask yourself, "Can I have all these emotions and questions and still be able to say that God is good?" Tindle suggests that we need to hold these seemingly contradictory issues in a kind of tension throughout our lives.

The Lord has continued to develop me, and I can now accept my illness and leave it in His hands. I have seen Him provide for every need throughout this miserable time and can believe He has a plan for my future. At this point, I have no obvious tumor. I will have no surgery. In six months or less I will know more and if I perish, I perish.

Trusting God is the key to accepting your condition as well as your failure to understand the reason for it. If you can trust God on the basis of His goodness and mercy and love, then you can be confident that, no matter what happens, He will always take care of you. No matter how bad life gets, God is in control, and there is something much better waiting for you.

As you move beyond "why" questions, you will be better able to consider the possible purposes of suffering. The next chapter presents several possibilities and offers biblical suggestions about how you can respond in faith to suffering.

————◆◆◆————

F

QUESTIONS TO ASK YOURSELF

There are questions you can ask that will help you move beyond "why" and focus on how God's character relates to your illness. You might want to take the time to write out your thoughts and reasons. Keep your answers to yourself or discuss them with a friend. If you save your notes, pull them out again in a few months and compare present answers to past ones. You might be surprised to find out that your responses have changed over time and through your new experiences.

- Do you believe that God is good and sovereign? If so, do you believe that only when your life is going well?

  _____

  _____

  _____

  _____

- Do you believe that God loves you and wants the best for you no matter what?

  _____

  _____

  _____

  _____

- Can you think of some ways in which God has specifically shown you His love in the past?

  _____

  _____

  _____

  _____

- Do you think these past events give any indication (or have any bearing) on how He will care for you in the present and the future?

  _____

  _____

  _____

  _____

- Are you feeling that life is unfair because of unmet expectations?

  _____

  _____

  _____

• Are your expectations realistic, or have you created a comfortable cocoon for yourself?

_____

_____

_____

_____

• How are you going to react now that you are not getting what you want out of life?

_____

_____

_____

_____

• Do you think God is powerful enough to heal you? Why or why not?

_____

_____

_____

_____

• Are you able to trust God with your physical illness and become confident that He will sustain you in spite of the outcome? If so, think of an example of when you did so.

_____

_____

_____

_____

• Are you part of the reason behind your suffering? Why or why not?

_____

_____

_____

• Are you struggling with envy, wishing you had what others
  have? If so, is this blocking acceptance of your situation? What
  can you do?

  _____

  _____

  _____

  _____

• What aspect of the "why" question do you struggle with the
  most?

  _____

  _____

  _____

  _____

• Where could you turn for encouragement or assistance with
  your questions?

  _____

  _____

  _____

  _____

My soul weeps because of grief;
Strengthen me according to Thy word.

PSALM 119:28

———◆◆◆———

F

What is the Christian answer to the mystery of suffering?
Not an explanation, but a reinforcing presence—Christ to stand
beside you through the darkness, Christ's companionship to make the
dark experience sacred. "Even though I walk through the valley of the
shadow of death, I fear no evil: for Thou art with me" (Psalm 23:4).

JAMES S. STEWART

FOUR

Worth All the Suffering

E ven as his blue eyes held back the welling tears, George Fiegel affirmed his belief that something good *can* come from something bad. George had walked the steps of diagnosis, treatments, and hospitalizations alongside his late wife, Jean, before she succumbed to an unsuccessful bone marrow transplant for non-Hodgkin's lymphoma.

George says that before his wife became ill, he was immature in his Christian faith. "Looking back over those difficult years, I see how much I've learned about myself and God," he says. "I have a new life [in Christ] now, and for that I am extremely thankful." He says that he wouldn't trade that unexpected blessing of growing closer to God. "I can feel God's spirit leading, and I have a strong desire to move in the way He wants me to move."

Now George can look back on his experience with sorrow-tinged contentment; but it didn't happen overnight or feel like a blessing while it was happening. Don't be surprised or discouraged if you are having a hard time believing that anything good could come from your situation. However, consider the possibilities if good *can* come from bad.

Why do some of us have such a painful life? Do those of us who have such struggles seek to grow in the Lord?

For years I strove to lay aside self and learn the disciplines of godliness, but I was never able to achieve even the smallest step toward my goal. Then I got cancer, and I began to grow. In reading Luke 11, it says that we will receive what we ask for. Yes, I am receiving it, but I never imagined it would mean I had to go through this!

WHAT SOCIETY SAYS ABOUT SUFFERING

In 1900, Americans could expect to live to the age of forty-seven. My dad never met his grandfather, who died in an iron mine accident in 1913 at the age of thirty-five. He never met his maternal grandmother, either. She died in childbirth in 1913 at the age of thirty-nine. The daughter she bore died of pneumonia when she was seven months old. Dad's aunt died of influenza in 1929 at the age of eighteen. Today, however, the average American can expect to live more than seventy-six years.

In modern American society, most people do not experience suffering as early, as often, or as severely as in earlier centuries. Improved nutrition, technology, and medical advances have not only dramatically increased the average lifespan; they have also isolated many Americans from regular encounters with sickness and pain. Many people now take good health for granted. Some never experience serious physical pain or illness throughout their longer lives. If they do get sick, they can choose from an array of medications to combat pain and physical symptoms, and technology can prolong their lives. Unlike most of the world's populations, most Americans today don't see death up close until late in life.

Then there is the case that suffering is part of the human condition. In our century, we often think that we can avoid pain and suffering by applying more technology to our

*medicine, and to a certain extent we can. However, our
ability to prolong life, in itself has produced more suffering
and sometimes extends the period of suffering. People now
live long enough to suffer from diseases of long-term dete-
rioration. We cannot eliminate suffering because it is part
of the terms of living after the Fall.... Are we more idealistic than other cultures or even our own past generations?*

*I think we are. We have been raised with so much
and have been protected from many of the realities of suffering and death. How many of us have seen a person
die?*

Philip Yancey says that modern society tends to view pain as an
unnecessary sensation that can and should be mastered by technology. He writes:

We moderns have isolated ourselves from a world [that]
claims pain as an integral part of it. In all of history, except
very recent times, pain was a normal, everyday occurrence,
which was taken for granted in any balanced view of life.
Now it is an adjunct, an intruder we must excise.[1]

*I suspect all of us have a part of us that thinks we are
immune to suffering. It is part of our overlying ideal-
ism.... When such a person, raised on the idealistic world
of the movies, faces pain or suffering, the initial reaction
is to escape it.*

In *Making Sense out of Suffering*, Peter Kreeft says that modern
society sees suffering as a problem to be conquered rather than a
mystery to be understood or a moral challenge to be embraced. He
observes a shift between the ancient mind and the modern:

At issue here is the important question in the world. What is the greatest good? What gives our lives meaning? What is our end? Modernity answers, feeling good. The ancients answer, being good. Feeling good is not compatible with suffering; being good is. Therefore the fact of suffering threatens modernity much more than it threatened the ancients.... So suffering does not refute belief in a good God to the ancient mind because a good God might well sacrifice our subjective happiness for our objective happiness. But the modern mind finds it hard to make that distinction; therefore, it finds it hard to believe in a good God who lets us suffer.[2]

In modern society many people conclude that suffering is without meaning because there is no apparent reason for it. Often this view feeds into the belief that life, too, is without an ultimate purpose. If you do not believe in a sovereign God who allowed this tragedy in your life, you will probably conclude that it happened simply by accident. Such randomness renders the entire experience meaningless.

What if you believe in God but restrict His power, goodness, or love? If so, a loving, personal God has nothing to do with your life. Again, the suffering has no inherent value because your god wasn't willing or able to prevent it. It is the result of unchecked laws of nature.

The God of the Bible, however, offers a place to lay out all the questions about suffering—at the foot of Jesus' cross. Christians do not have to run away from suffering, because Christ provides the key to turning it into a blessing.

At this time, I could not see what would happen in the months and years that followed. Yes, my world had been turned upside-down and the life that was to follow was not as I had planned, but ahead was a time of the most

*incredible growth which was worth all the suffering
which produced it.*

WHAT THE BIBLE SAYS ABOUT SUFFERING

According to Kreeft, the Cross is the context that explains suffering:

> For the darkest door of all has been shoved open and light
> from beyond it has streamed into our world to light our
> way, since He has changed the meaning of death. It is not
> merely that He rose from the dead, but that He changed the
> meaning of death, and therefore also all the little deaths, all
> the sufferings that anticipate death and make up part of
> it…. But He came into life and death, and He still comes.
> He is still here…with us, taking our blows. Every tear we
> shed becomes His tear. He may not *yet* wipe them away, but
> He makes them His…. Thus God's answer to the problem
> of suffering not only happened 2,000 years ago, but it is still
> happening in our lives. The solution to our suffering is our
> suffering! All our suffering can become part of His work, the
> greatest work ever done….[3]

Believing that Christ, as Kreeft writes, "transformed death from
a hole into a door, from an end into a beginning" is paramount
when you are faced with a serious illness. Christ has promised
never to forsake or leave you. If you are a Christian, it is ultimately
impossible for you to lose your battle for wellness because whether
you live or die, you are the Lord's (see Romans 14:8; John
11:25–26).

In light of this, you have a choice to make: You can either accept
what God has allowed in your life and use it for His glory, or you
can reject His will for your life out of fear, denial, or anger.

Therefore, if we can accept the possibility of a God who cares for His creation and has created the world for a purpose, then we open up the door for a life that has meaning. In this case, we are here to prepare for another life—an eternal one. If, in fact, God created an intelligent life form who had free will so that he could choose for God or against God, then the life on this planet is designed to set the stage for the development of this decision.

There would be no real decision if it were laid out in such a way that one direction was totally ugly and the other was totally beautiful. The complexity of the world in which we live makes it an interesting choice. We are given the opportunity to think that we are in control so that we can decide whether we want to be in control or if we are willing to relinquish that control to God.

If you choose to accept your situation, you can see more readily how God places hedges around His people for their protection (see Job 1:6–10). Margaret Clarkson says that God has made a hedge about the life of every believer:

> The thorns that seem to hem us in are in reality placed there to close us in to God Himself, to protect us from evil, to provide us with sanctuary in the midst of a troubled world…. For most of His children, God's hedges do not seemingly entail suffering, but only protection. For some, however, they mean unending pain and weakness, disappointment and sorrow, varying in degree to total imprisonment. Why this must be so, we may not know; sufficient for us to know that God Himself has hedged us in, and God's hedges are always hedges of protection and blessing. And God Himself, living there both with us and in us, longs to make of our thorny wall a thing of wonder to men and angels and

demons, a thing that will one day bring forth holy blossom and fruit to our eternal good and His eternal glory.[4]

How might God be working through your suffering to refine you for His eternal purposes? Here are several biblical possibilities. As you study and pray about them, ask God to show you how to use your suffering for His glory.[5]

Suffering enables you to honor God.

Your words, actions, and attitudes paint a picture of your relationship with God. They can bring Him either honor or dishonor. They can be either a good example to others or a bad one. Do you remember what Job said when his family and all his worldly goods were suddenly gone? "The Lord gave and the Lord has taken away. Blessed be the name of the Lord" (Job 1:21; see also 1 Peter 1:6–7).

Suffering demonstrates God's power.

It's only when you are weak—that is, not dependent upon yourself—that you can be strong in Christ. "Most gladly, therefore, I will rather boast about my weakness," wrote the apostle Paul, "that the power of Christ may dwell in me...for when I am weak, then I am strong" (2 Corinthians 12:9–10).

Suffering allows God to give His grace.

Three times Paul asked God to remove his "thorn in the flesh." God's answer was: "My grace is sufficient for you" (2 Corinthians 12:8–9; see also 1 Corinthians 15:10; Ephesians 4:7; Philippians 2:13; 1 Peter 5:10).

Suffering prepares you to help others.

In 2 Corinthians 1:3–5, Paul tells the believers at Corinth that God is the God of all comfort and that they share not only His sufferings, but also His comfort. Because God will comfort you in the midst of your suffering, you will be able to comfort others with the same comfort and give them hope.

> *I have forgotten that there is no time wasted if we view each thing which comes to us, as from the Lord. So it is with my new instructions. He gave me the doctor who in turn got me into the NIH. So this new suffering is from the Lord—whatever it entails. I must face it with joy, utilizing this opportunity to serve Him, reaching out to the people He sends to me.*

Suffering helps build character.

Think of one person you admire deeply. Why do you think that person has such great character? Often, though not always, the people with the greatest character have experienced tragedies or walked a path of suffering. Their life experiences have shaped them into something quite beautiful. How does this happen? Paul wrote to the believers in Rome: "We also exult in our tribulations, knowing that tribulation brings about perseverance; and perseverance, proven character; and proven character, hope; and hope does not disappoint, because the love of God has been poured out within our hearts through the Holy Spirit who has been given to us"(Romans 5:3–5).

> *As I studied the Scriptures and read numerous books on the subject of pain and suffering, I began to recognize my faulty thinking. The Scriptures are filled with the pain and suffering of God's people. Some of God's most powerful servants suffered the most. For example, the apostle Paul had a long list of the suffering he endured as he tried to spread the Good News.*

Suffering encourages you to trust God.

Children trust much more easily than adults do. Too often, children grow up to be self-sufficient, independent adults who don't "need" God in their lives. Yet, Jesus reminded His disciples that the kingdom of heaven belongs to children (Matthew 19:14), and God calls us to "be imitators of God, as beloved children" (Ephesians 5:1). In 2 Corinthians 1:9–10, Paul makes it very clear that he needed God and that he trusted in Him: "Indeed, we had the sentence of death within ourselves in order that we should not trust in ourselves, but in God who raises the dead; who delivered us from so great a peril of death, and will deliver us, He on whom we have set our hope. And He will yet deliver us."

> *Guidance: God promises to guide us. So why is it sometimes so difficult to trust His way? Think back to His former guidance. As I went through various trials, I could see His hand. Now I look back and want to explain things naturally. Surely He brought me through the initial crisis. For a while I thought He might have planned for me to have won. But not so. I am to fight again. I am to go through more miseries. I am ready to die. But I do not know who else I am to minister to in the process. He will guide me if I will follow. He will give me the strength to meet every challenge.*

Suffering helps you learn to thank God and praise Him in everything.

First Thessalonians 5:16, 18 tells us to "Rejoice always…in everything gives thanks; for this is God's will for you in Christ Jesus." Without a doubt, this is a hard task! Margaret Clarkson suggests a few ways to praise God in the midst of suffering: Praise God for Himself, His sovereignty, wisdom, never-failing mercies and compassion, love, grace, holiness, justice, and power. She recommends meditating on Scripture to help cultivate a response of praise.

Suffering helps you identify with Christ's suffering.

How often do you stop to think about how much Christ suffered for you? He died for you while you were still a sinner and saved you from the wrath of God (Romans 5:8–9). Read through the entire chapter of Isaiah 53 and list all the words that describe what Christ suffered for you (for example, *pierced, afflicted, forsaken*). How does your own suffering change your perspective on what Christ did for you? (See also Romans 8:17–18; Philippians 1:29; 3:10; 2 Thessalonians 1:5.)

Suffering helps you partake of God's holiness.

You have the honor and privilege of sharing in the inheritance of the saints because God the Father has qualified you (Colossians 1:12). Paul says that he does all things for the sake of the gospel so that he may become a fellow partaker of it (1 Corinthians 9:23). And Peter reminds us that being a fellow partaker of sufferings also means that we will partake of the glory that is to be revealed (1 Peter 4:12–16; 5:1). Never forget that God's "precious and magnificent promises" have made you a partaker of the divine nature (2 Peter 1:4).

Suffering offers you the chance to reflect on God's discipline.

It is possible that God has allowed this suffering in your life so that you will learn from it. Punishment is not in view here—only a divine, purposeful opportunity for growth and change. God's discipline, unlike that of an earthly parent, is perfect and will yield the peaceful fruit of righteousness so that you can share in His holiness (Hebrews 12:8–13).

Our worst fears were realized as the doctor told us the cancer is in the liver. Yesterday I think I was mostly in shock. Today I can assess the damage and find reason for much hope and rejoicing. For this I was born! Some people live to serve. I must learn to reach outward—away from my pain—to help others with theirs. I am free of a job and must learn to use my time wisely.

Some of these purposes of suffering may seem difficult or impossible for you to accept right now. As you continue to think about them, cling to the incredible promise of 1 Peter 5:10: "And after you have suffered for a little, the God of all grace, who called you to His eternal glory in Christ, will Himself perfect, confirm, strengthen and establish you." God Himself will take care of all the details of perfecting, confirming, strengthening, and establishing you as you walk the painful road of suffering.

KEEPING THE FAITH

Even in the midst of extreme physical suffering, a heightened sensitivity to God's hand in your life can bring you joy and peace as you watch Him work. God will not only sustain you; He will also bless you in ways you never could have thought of. These blessings may or may not be physical ones.

As the weeks went by, I began to see something unexpected. In spite of all the misery I was in because of the chemotherapy, there were also blessings. Usually, they were small things about which I had worried that were resolved in a way that I never could have imagined.

Worry about the future, especially financial stability, continually crept into my mom's mind, and her anxiety frequently interfered with her ability to enjoy life. Not long after she became ill, the medical bills multiplied, seemingly overnight. She had always had to struggle against worrying about money, and in this situation, I feared she would be overcome. But God blessed her tremendously!

> *I have been thinking for days about all that I have learned in the past year. Most important, I think, has been the ability now to leave things in the Lord's hands. I realize that for the first time in my life, I do not look at life as "too hard." I am actually enjoying things— enjoying each day.*

There are several things you can do to keep your circumstances from overwhelming your faith. The most important is to keep your focus on Jesus. The minute your gaze drifts away, becomes distracted, or locks onto something or someone else, you can sink beneath the waves of doubt, fear, and hopelessness.

> *My problem is that I am not good at turning away from my thoughts. I need to practice focusing on the Lord and on others.*

Keeping your focus on Jesus is an act of your will, a conscious decision made daily, if not hourly. You need to resolve to look to Him as your source of strength. He is your ultimate priority.

> *My goal is to really know God—to know His character, to seek His will as I have never sought it before. It is no simple thing I endeavor for I desire to walk within His kingdom.*

Remember that going through trials requires only a small amount of faith, exercised a little bit at a time. God will take care of us and fill in the gaps. My mom recorded her discovery of this simple truth.

This morning I was moving the mound of dirt that used to be garden and was sort of laughing about how you move a mountain—shovelful by shovelful. Then as I was going to relate this joke to Dave a thought struck me concerning the Scripture: if we have the faith of a grain of mustard seed, we can move mountains (Matthew 17:20). I think we move mountains through a long, continuing faith, which sees us through each shovelful—not a big blast of faith that lifts the entire mountain in one bunch, as I once thought.

Although fixing your eyes firmly on Jesus is most important, there are other things you can do that will help you persevere in your faith.

- Read at least one psalm every day.
- Pray constantly, whether you're at home, in a hospital or waiting room, stopped at a red light, or waiting in line at a grocery store.
- Ask other people to pray for you. This will give you more strength to persevere than you could ever imagine.
- Keep a journal. Track God's answers to your prayers as well as His daily blessings. (On a bleak day, reading through your journal will encourage you.)
- Lean on God's Word—not your own understanding—in every situation.
- Thank God for His daily blessings of the little things in life.

RESPONDING IN FAITH

As a pastor, Bill Hill studied and knew intellectually the tenets of Christian faith. Now he's had three years of experiential learning. "What is exciting is that all the things I've preached academically throughout my lifetime are really working in my life," he says.

Fighting cancer and faced with his own mortality, Hill says that turning his suffering around to glorify God and encourage other people has helped keep his mind off of his illness.

Hill remembers one night in the hospital, when, listening to the never-ending sounds of activity, for three hours he wrestled with *all* of his questions. "I had a peace that night after the three hours of struggle, and I was willing to accept whatever happened to me," he says. "I can actually say now that I am thrilled that God has given me this ministry."

In Mark 1 Jesus begins His ministry. One after another receives healing or deliverance. People are continually drawn to Him. What is my ministry? I am not in this position for nothing.

Dietrich Bonhoeffer, who was martyred during World War II, says that whoever avoids suffering also throws away God's greatest gifts:

> The tribulation that seems so harsh and abhorrent in our lives is in truth full of the most wonderful treasures a Christian can find. It is like an oyster with a pearl inside, like a deep mine shaft in which one finds one metal after another the deeper one descends into it: first ore, then silver, and finally gold. Suffering produces patience, and then experience, and then hope.[6]

In his sermon "Wearing the Thorns As a Crown," James S. Stewart says: "The true Christian reaction to suffering and sorrow is not the attitude of self-pity or fatalism or resentment: it is the spirit which takes life's difficulties as a God-given opportunity, and regards its troubles as a sacred trust, and wears the thorns as a crown."[7]

How do you come to the place where you accept your suffering and wear your "thorns" as a crown? First, you can choose to allow God to use you despite your illness. This is a choice only you can make. Second, you can believe that God allowed you to experience this specific illness for a good reason. (This took me an extremely long time to believe in my head, let alone in my heart.) Third, you can respond to your illness purposefully—in relation to God, to yourself, and to others. Others have gone before to show you the way.

When she was in her eighties, Corrie ten Boom suffered a stroke, and then another, and another. She had spent years writing books and traveling around the world sharing the lessons God had taught her in Nazi concentration camps. Now the strokes had robbed her of her mobility and her ability to speak. Nevertheless, she continued her ministry: Her eyes revealed her silent intercession and love for those around her.

Corrie's friend and companion, Pamela Rosewell Moore, said of her: "She had served Him in her youth; now she was serving Him in her old age. She had served Him in strength, now she was serving Him in weakness. She had served Him in health; she was serving Him in illness."[8] Corrie pushed forward with the abilities she still had. She could not write books or speak anymore, but she could still pray for people. She could no longer travel, but she could still minister to those in her household.

Ultimately, you and your life are in the palm of God's hand. Whether you live or die, you are the Lord's (Romans 14:8), and you can exalt Him in your body, both in life and in death (Philippians 1:20). What an incredible adventure lies ahead of you—the opportunity to glorify God with your suffering and pain!

——————

F

BIBLICAL RESPONSES TO SUFFERING

Below are some biblical responses to suffering. Read through them and think about how they might help you persevere in faith in your health situation.

- Hope and trust in the Lord (Job 13:15).
- Thank God for His presence in your valley (Psalm 23:4).
- Realize that God is with you always, wherever you go (Psalm 23:4–6).
- Cast your burdens on Him (Psalm 55:22).
- Look to (and ask) God for guidance (Psalm 73:23–26).
- Fear the Lord (Psalm 103:13–14).
- Walk out in faith (Isaiah 43:2).
- Comfort others just as God has comforted you (2 Corinthians 1:3–4).
- Desire heaven (2 Corinthians 5:2; Colossians 3:2) and God's presence more and more (Psalm 42:1; John 15:4).
- Rejoice and give praise, glory, and honor to Jesus (1 Thessalonians 5:16; 1 Peter 1:6–7; James 1:2–4).
- Pray (James 5:13).
- Patiently endure your suffering (1 Peter 2:19–24).
- Follow Christ's example of suffering (1 Peter 2:19–24).
- Live for the will of God (1 Peter 4:1–2).
- Glorify God (1 Peter 4:16).
- Entrust your soul to God, the faithful Creator (1 Peter 4:19).
- Do what is right (1 Peter 4:19).
- Cast all your anxiety on Him because He cares for you (1 Peter 5:7).

PART II

MAKING THE TURN

Working on C. S. Lewis' <u>Mere Christianity</u> last night, ran across a most significant thought—one I do not wish to lose sight of again. "Every time you make a choice you are turning the central part of you, the part that chooses, into something a little different from what it was before."

This makes <u>today</u> significant for today I am going to change for the better or the worse. Too often I have felt that I am treading water, waiting for something to come along that makes my life worthwhile when in fact, each moment of each day is significant.

I get the same sense of daily growth from 2 Corinthians 5:16–18: "Inner man is being renewed day by day. Momentary light affliction is producing for us an eternal weight of glory..." Praise Him for this daily growth.

I would have despaired unless
I had believed that I would
see the goodness of the LORD
in the land of the living.
Wait for the LORD;
Be strong, and let your heart take courage;
Yes, wait for the LORD.

PSALM 27:13–14

———◆◆◆———

F

There are things in life which are irreparable,
there is no road back to yesterday.

OSWALD CHAMBERS

A Practical Plan

I n his mind, Eugene Clark ran his fingers over the organ keys, playing his cantata again and again until he was confident that it was perfect. It had been several years since he had played a real organ.

Blind and bedridden at the age of thirty-eight, Eugene had wondered how he would be able to financially support his wife and their three young children. As he lay in bed, he gave a great deal of thought to how he could continue to arrange and compose music. All he had to do was figure out how to get the notes on paper—and he did. For nineteen years, Eugene worked from his bed. Friends, neighbors, and coworkers all commented on his unwavering faith in God despite his difficult circumstances.[1]

You, too, might live with your illness for a long, long time. If you have been diagnosed with a life-threatening illness, your life *has changed forever*. It will never be the same again. You, too, will need to make changes in your life to accommodate your condition. The pieces of your life may look so broken now that you think you cannot make the adjustment. Even though it won't be easy, you *can* do it.

After the initial period of your health crisis passes, you can attempt to assess your new life, perhaps with the help of a family member or good friend. Which pieces of your life are still intact? Which have been damaged? Which ones are missing? Once you have determined that, you can begin to accommodate, adjust, and adapt to your illness.

PICKING UP THE PIECES

How do you adjust to something that affects every facet of your life and threatens to engulf your schedule, lifestyle, and even your relationships?

First, remember that change is a part of life. It is simply one of those constants. Things never stay the same for very long, and, however hard it may seem at first, it's always best to adapt to change instead of clinging to what once was.

Although a serious illness may appear to be the single most formidable obstacle you have ever experienced, in essence, it's just another change. It will, without a doubt, challenge your ability to adapt. It will test your strength, courage, and creativity; and it will stretch your patience, endurance, and personal limits. Still, don't underestimate yourself or your family as you look for new ways to adapt to your condition.

If you feel that you're not ready to take a step toward adjustment right now, keep trying to work through your emotions. Individuals are unique and therefore require different amounts of time to deal with their initial responses. Remember, you probably won't wake up one morning and think, *Hey, I am all done with feeling these feelings, so now it's time to adapt to what has happened to me.* Emotions and feelings will always be part of the package, so don't wait for them to disappear before you take steps to accommodate your situation.

Irene Pollin compares the adjustment to an illness to the ebb and flow of the tides. This uneven, rhythmic tidal motion pushes forward and then pulls back as part of a continuous cycle. "Since the course of many chronic illnesses is unpredictable, adjustment and accommodation today doesn't mean that you've conquered tomorrow's problems," says Pollin. "If you buy into that, you'll constantly find yourself at the mercy of your illness. The trick is to cope with every situation as it occurs, no matter where it takes you. If you expect the unexpectable, you—and not your illness—will be in charge of your life."[2]

Dr. Daniel Haffey agrees that adjusting to a serious illness is not a linear process. Reality breaks through regularly, causing emotional setbacks. Therefore, you need to be prepared for a wild ride with unpredictable turns, stops, and switchbacks. Expecting the unexpected will reduce your stress and increase your ability to cope.

Although your new life will be unpredictable in many ways, the good news is that there are some strategies you can use to cope with some of the daily stress and strain.

COPING STRATEGIES

Get Involved with Your Health Care

Getting involved with your health care can be a significant way to facilitate adjustment. Mary Raymer strongly recommends that a patient *take charge* of all the things he can, especially his own health. A patient who participates actively in his health care feels more in control of what is happening to him.

"Remember that health-care workers are there to help you; they are *not* there to tell you what to do," Raymer emphasizes. "They are there to support you, give you the information you need, and present you with all your options; but they are not there to control your life. If you are not getting this, you should feel free to go elsewhere." You, and only you, are responsible for making decisions about your health, unless you become incapacitated.

My mom spent quite a bit of time at the National Library of Medicine in Bethesda, Maryland, researching ovarian cancer. (This was before the Internet.) She learned as much as possible about her illness and kept abreast of studies on new treatments and protocols.

Her research helped her make more informed decisions about her treatment. She also became acquainted with cancer terminology and technical lingo, which helped her communicate better with her physician.

> *My doctor had adamantly refused to give me the statistics of my diagnosis for fear that it would somehow prevent me from developing a positive attitude. Yet, it seemed to work contrary to what my doctor expected—for the less I knew, the more I anticipated the worst.*
>
> *Once I knew that 30 percent of ovarian cancer patients lived five years, I was encouraged that there were so many! It was also encouraging to see all the work that was being done in the area of cancer research and some of the developments, which had come out of this research in recent years.*

In some cases, patients will be unable to be active participants. In that case, spouses or other family members may become responsible for making decisions on their behalf. These family members may also feel more in control of the situation because they are so involved.

"Researching Alzheimer's disease was great therapy for me," says Glenn Kirkland, whose wife, Grace, was diagnosed early with that incurable disease. "The doctors said there was nothing to be done, period. Well, I wanted to do everything I could for Grace, and I didn't leave any stone unturned."

Both he and Grace participated in research at the National Institutes of Health (NIH) and at Johns Hopkins University, and even though nothing helped his wife's condition or stopped the progression of her disease, he considers the experience invaluable. "With the help of Johns Hopkins, an advocacy group was formed in Baltimore, and I found myself president. I quickly discovered that I was not alone, by any means." Getting involved on Grace's behalf led Glenn to work on behalf of many others. He now acts as a consultant to a number of groups seeking to serve the disadvantaged elderly.[3]

Only you can determine the level and extent of your involvement with your own or your loved one's health care. Some may just want to read a few books or pamphlets about their illness, whereas others will gain great satisfaction from learning as much as they can. Any amount of involvement can be beneficial to you as you become more educated about your condition and get in touch with others in similar situations. You, too, may be able to reach out to others in your community and educate them about your particular illness.

Choose Your Team

Your physician and staff are now significant people in your life. Although medical decisions are entirely yours to make, you want the best doctor available. You need to be able to work with your doctor as you choose the best treatments or therapies and cope with any potential side effects.

Natalie Davis Springarn suggests that patients use the following criteria when selecting a doctor:

- basic credentials,
- board certification,
- experience,
- type of practice,
- office procedure,
- hospital affiliation,
- nursing and paraprofessionals,
- rapport with patients,
- office atmosphere,
- the doctor's manner and style.[4]

Family members and friends should remember that medical decisions are entirely at the discretion of the patient. They need to respect choices made and offer advice only when the patient specifically requests it.

I knew that I had two sources in which to turn, sources which in some ways are the antithesis of one another. My scientific sources told me to seek as much help from the scientific and medical community that I could, and my spiritual source told me simply to trust in the Lord and He would bring me through this challenge. I decided that I could not turn my back on either for I considered that both came from the same source, God.

God had given the knowledge which was now being applied to the treatment of the disease, and I would draw upon this as long as possible. I felt that Jesus' response to the question of taxes applied here. He said to "give unto Caesar the things which are Caesar's and to God the things which are God's."

In this case I was using the expertise of the doctors of this world to deal with the treatment of a disease of this world and would rely on God for the spiritual aspects of my reaction and struggle. This attitude coincided with my perception that ultimately God was in control of all aspects of my treatment, but I had to have a practical plan for following Him.

The plan I chose was that I would follow the directions of the doctor, believing that she was the spokesperson for God. It was a good choice, though not without its discomforts. It meant submitting to the most devastating of treatments, but by deciding to follow the doctor's plans, it meant never giving in to thoughts of quitting the plan to receive six successive treatments, three weeks apart. In the midst of severe suffering, such thoughts were common and for the comfort of the moment, the effectiveness of the treatments could have been compromised by their early termination.

A challenging question faces many who have been diagnosed with a potentially life-threatening illness: What about choosing alternative medical treatments? This is a question that goes far beyond the scope of this book and involves a decision that only you can make. However, it is important to discuss all possible treatments with your physician before you begin any treatment, including "natural" remedies. Alternative medicine can contain pharmacoactive agents, which may or may not be helpful. The danger lies in the possibility that different active substances can cause a wide variety of effects.

Keep in mind that you may be at a vulnerable point in your decision-making process and that not everyone has your best interests at heart. "There are times when advocates of alternative medicine can prey on this vulnerability," says Dr. David L. Stevens. "Some will influence the patient to stop all allopathic medicine interventions and just follow their recommendations."[5]

Charting the Journey gives several guidelines to follow if you're considering alternative medicine or unconventional treatments.[6]

- Be sure you understand your unconventional treatment thoroughly.
- Find out at the very beginning whether any unconventional treatment you're considering can be used in addition to whatever traditional treatments you're considering.
- Check out the unconventional practitioner's credentials and the conditions under which he practices.

- Find out the track record of the unconventional treatment.
- Be sure you know how much the unconventional treatment costs.
- Ask yourself if you are comfortable with the treatment in question.
- Before you make any decision about alternative medicine treatments, consult the many resources available and research all the possibilities.

Watch Your Emotional Health

It's also essential to learn about the emotional aspects of an illness, says Raymer, who encourages all patients to consider using the services of mental health practitioners. "We all need support when we are grieving a loss," she says. "Not all of us need psychotherapy, but all of us need validation and information. It is better to have someone to listen to us who is objective and who can evaluate whether we've crossed over from normal grief into a more complicated one."

Too often, a patient is referred to a mental health-care worker only when he falls apart during a checkup. But, as Raymer points out, that hardly ever happens. "A patient or family member typically experiences a major emotional upheaval *after* he leaves the doctor's office; that is, in the car or at home." She says that being seen by a counselor, social worker, or psychologist can help, even if you go only once. "The definition that knowledge is power is true, especially in the case of a serious illness," she says. She recommends that patients and families not wait until they think there is a "problem" before seeking out a mental health-care professional.[7]

Reevaluate Your Work

It's hard enough to handle work responsibilities when you are healthy, let alone when you are dealing with a major health crisis. If you are employed, you may wonder what you should do about your job. If you are in school, you may question whether or not you can still attend classes. This is an area you will have to reevaluate at different stages of your illness.

In *Diagnosis Cancer,* Wendy Schlessel Harpham says that there are several questions a patient should ask before heading back to work or school:

- How flexible is my work or school schedule?
- How demanding is my job, both physically and emotionally?
- How well am I doing physically?
- How well am I doing emotionally?
- Will I be at increased risk for serious infection in my work or school environment?[8]

You should certainly discuss your job or school situation with your doctor and your family. You may need to take a short or long leave of absence or perhaps reduce your hours. Your family and friends could help you discern if your job or school career meshes comfortably with your illness.

They might also be willing to partner with you if you wish to stay employed. If you cannot drive, for example, family members, friends, neighbors, or coworkers could take turns carpooling with you. Your employer could also be an ally. There might be new possibilities, either in work hours or job assignments, that could help you do your job more efficiently.

That was the longest summer of my life. Every three weeks I would return to the hospital for another dose of poison to try to destroy the deadly tumors. With each treatment, the side effects became worse, yet I would still try to go to work as much as possible. It was the only way I could try to cling to some sort of normalcy in a life that had become fully out of control. The nausea was with me constantly. I could never enjoy a meal. The only release I found was during sleep. I had so little energy that I had to plan my day very carefully, making sure that I conserved my strength for necessary activities.

Once you have your physician's approval, the decision to work can be made at your discretion. If you are in the process of deciding whether or not to continue working, you must factor in many variables. To help you weigh the pros and cons of employment, look over the following chart. You may want to add a few of your own needs and concerns.

P R O	C O N
• It will have financial compensation. • It will give you a sense of normalcy. • It will keep you from feeling isolated. • It will keep your work skills current. • It will give you a sense of satisfaction.	• Your illness and its side effects may become more public. • You may spend all your "good hours" at work, taking time away from your family. • You may not have the strength or energy to do the same job.

Remember that working full-time is only one of your options. You might want to consider working part-time, retiring early, or taking a leave of absence.

Marguerite Henry Atkins's husband, Dick, kept working for as long as possible after he was diagnosed with Alzheimer's disease. Since Dick was in his midfifties, Marguerite talked with his employer, and together they helped Dick continue working until he could take early retirement. After he retired, Dick became restless, and Marguerite began to look around for something that would help fill the void. Finally, a friend who managed a small furniture store gave him a job working two half-days a week. This job gave Dick a feeling of being involved, and he was proud to be earning some money again.[9]

Did you know that resources are available to help your employer accommodate you in your illness? The Job Accommodation Network (JAN), a free service of the President's Committee on Employment for the Handicapped, was established in 1984 to provide information about practical job accommodations. JAN is an international, toll-free consulting service that provides information about job accommodations and the employability of people with functional limitations.[10]

> For six months, I survived with few moments of relief from the nausea which gripped me almost constantly. With each treatment, the side effects became worse as the chemicals built up in my system. I struggled to return to work, for there I discovered I had something to occupy my mind. My coworker was also a great encourager, who would not let me give in to depression. After each treatment, I was bedridden for a week. The next two weeks were an attempt at pretending that chemotherapy did not exist.

Pace Yourself

Fatigue and weariness are common symptoms of many serious illnesses, due either to the side effects of treatment or to the disease itself. Fatigue can cause you to miss workdays, make it difficult for you to socialize with friends or be intimate with your spouse, and interfere with your daily activities. Therefore, it is extremely important that you learn how to pace yourself.

Raymer says that patients usually try to cram too much activity into a "good" day. The result, she says, is an increase in "bad" days. "Even though you might be feeling well, you should not try to do a lot of extra things during these 'feeling good' moments. You will become worn down again, bringing on a bad day." She recommends that you carefully pace yourself even on your good days. Restraining yourself in this way takes a large amount of self-discipline, especially if you have a Type A personality.

So, how do you pace yourself? The most important thing you can do is to identify and set your priorities. This process is so important that the next chapter is devoted to it. Here are some other things you can do.

Talk with your mental health-care professional.

Describe symptoms of fatigue and ask for ways to alleviate them. You could keep a daily log of them. By noting their intensity and the timing of occurrence, a pattern may become evident.

Give yourself a reality check.

You need to continually ask yourself, *Does this really need to be done today?* Oftentimes, the answer may be no. You may also need to remind yourself that you will not be able to accomplish the same amount of things you once could—period. As long as you focus on what is most important to you, you will still be satisfied with what you do.

Make sure you get a balance of rest, play, and work.

Try to stay as physically rested as possible. You may need to go to bed earlier and take a nap during the day. Short naps and breaks may be more effective than long rest periods. Besides rest and work (whatever that work may be), it's important to add fun diversions to your day. Find something to do that is enjoyable and relaxing. My mom started knitting again after her cancer diagnosis. She said the rhythm of the needles relaxed her, and she felt satisfaction at the growing pile of finished outfits for a grandchild yet to be born.

Combine good eating habits with light exercise.

You should follow the dietary recommendations of your health-care team. If you have any questions or need help planning your menus, you should talk with a nutritionist familiar with your particular dietary needs. You may want to try eating small meals and snacks throughout the day instead of several large meals. Also, with the approval of your doctor, get some exercise. Take a walk in a park or just stroll around your neighborhood. If you are facing a more serious physical handicap, find out what your options are for exercise and physical therapy.

Be aware of how your energy level changes throughout the day.

When do you feel most energized? Can you predict when you need to rest? Once you are comfortable with your pattern, you will be able to plan activities to coincide with the times you have the most energy. You can even plan times to rest in between activities. In this way, you can make the most of your day.

> *Within a week of the operation, I was given my first of six chemotherapy treatments. As the chemicals poisoned my body, I was moved from the world of the living into a sort of shadow world where it was all that I could do to just draw the next breath.*

Family members should follow these same steps, especially as they take on additional responsibilities. They can help their ill loved one pace himself by modeling a well-paced lifestyle. If they run around frantically from one activity to another, they might find their loved one mirroring their behavior. They should try to be relaxed and attentive to their loved one, thereby helping him set a realistic, healthy pace.

Express Your Thoughts and Feelings

In 1871, while grieving the recent death of his son, Horatio Gates Spafford suffered financial disaster in the great Chicago fire. Spafford decided to take his wife and four daughters to England, and his wife and daughters left ahead of him on another ship. Soon he received a telegram from his wife saying that the ship had sunk and that all four of his daughters had drowned. When Spafford sailed, the captain pointed out the exact spot in the Atlantic Ocean where his daughters' ship had gone down. That night Spafford wrote the words for the hymn "It Is Well With My Soul":

> When peace like a river attendeth my way,
> When sorrows like sea-billows roll;
> Whatever my lot,
> Thou hast taught me to say,
> "It is well, it is well with my soul."

Writing is a powerful tool of expression. While you may not be inclined to pen a hymn, you can try your hand at writing about your life experience. You certainly don't have to be a professional writer to funnel your thoughts into words, and this creative outlet can be beneficial as you think through what you're up against. What safer place could there be to discover your beliefs and feelings about your illness than in a quiet corner with a notebook?

You may not know what to write about or even where you should start. To jump-start your journal writing, take a look at the following incomplete sentences. There are no right answers, and you don't have to show what you've written to anyone unless you choose to.

The overriding emotion that I feel right now is

_____

I am most bothered by

_____

The hardest thing for me to accept is

_____

Why don't people

_____

One thing I wish I could do right now is

_____

My life feels like

_____

I feel lucky when

_____

What makes me feel strong is

_____

I get frustrated when

_____

If I could turn back time, I would relive

_____

My favorite time of day is_____. It reminds me of

_____

I think God is

_____

Talking with a trusted friend or family member is also an excellent way to cope mentally with your illness. Not only can you share worries, frustrations, and fears about the present, but you also can reminisce about common experiences, laugh at mutual inside jokes, and just spend time together.

Remember that communicating with other people does not always involve speaking. It can also be in the form of a hand squeeze, a tight hug, a kiss, a backrub, or a light touch on the shoulder. Family members and friends should be especially conscious of using this kind of supportive communication.

If you have always depended on yourself to solve problems, you may find it difficult to broach the subject of your illness or talk openly about your emotions. This may be one area in which you might want to risk involving others. Try to identify at least one family member or friend with whom you can share honestly. You may, in fact, have to be the one to bring up the topic of how you are *really* feeling about your experience. Then you can decide what you want to say, how you want to say it, and when you want to say it. It's totally up to you. Purposefully expressing your emotions can help you cope with your situation.

On the other hand, you may have no trouble at all talking about your illness with others. In fact, without even realizing it, you might pour out your most negative thoughts and feelings to just about everyone. While it is essential to confide in a close friend, spouse, or other family member, it's probably wiser to refrain from doing this with every person who comes to visit.

"People who are in pain should try not to exhaust the nonprimary people in their lives," cautions Dr. Gilbert R. Gonzales. "If you want people to continue interacting with you and get close to you, try not to push them away with your constant complaining."[11] You can be selective about how much and to whom you complain. "The whole purpose of family is to provide continuing emotional support, especially when someone is ill," says Gonzales. But you should remain considerate of their feelings and struggles and not take them for granted.

For more help in this area, consider attending a support group or talking with a social worker, counselor, chaplain, pastor, or psychologist.

Cultivate a Cheerful Heart

Even though some people are just more serious than others, learning how to look at life a bit less seriously can lighten up any situation. A patient can often help set a tone of playfulness and laughter in the midst of circumstances that are very *unfunny*.

My mom did that.

She was waiting for him—the tall gentleman who stepped gingerly to her side of the hospital room. It was her coworker's first visit after hearing about the cancer diagnosis.

"Hi, Nancy. How are you?" he said awkwardly, trying not to look at all the paraphernalia in the room.

"Oh, fine. They take pretty good care of me here," she said.

After a few minutes of small talk, beeps erupted from my mom's IV machine. Looking worried, she quickly rummaged through her bedside stand.

"*Argh!* I don't have any left. Do you have some quarters? This thing only takes quarters. Hurry, it's about to beep again," she said.

A look of horror passed over her visitor's face as he plunged his hands deep into his pants pockets. "What? These things run off of coins? And they expect you and other patients to keep plopping them in? That's terrible. What is our world coming to, anyway?" he almost shouted, racing to the machine and looking in vain for a slot.

Finally, my mom could no longer control her smile. Her blue eyes twinkled. He immediately figured it out and joined in her laughter. "You sure got me that time!" he said, laughing again and feeling much more at ease.

My mom's love for pranks continued throughout her illness, and her sense of humor, I believe, helped alleviate tension and worry during tense situations. She poked fun at medical procedures that had to be done and playfully kept nurses guessing riddles.

If you cannot imagine making jokes or pulling pranks, that's fine. But you can figure out what you enjoy laughing about. What is funny to you? Do you like movies, cartoons, joke books, or comedians? Why not select a few videos and invite a few friends over for a "comedy night"?

Instead of watching shows or movies, consider having a storytelling session with some friends or your family. Each person takes turns sharing his or her own "funniest or most embarrassing moment." This never fails to get giggles from everyone.

Have you ever thought of humor as a way to cope with your illness? My mom knew that her hair was about to fall out due to chemotherapy, so she dyed her hair an obnoxious orange and headed to work. She wanted to make a transition to wearing her new wig. Coworkers were able to laugh *with* her that day and empathize with her impending loss.

After one chemotherapy regime was over, her hair started growing back. It's hard to wear a wig when the hair reaches a certain length, because it gets hot and itchy. She put the wig away. The new hair looked fuzzy and was extremely soft. She would invite people to touch her hair and "pet" her head. Soon no one even noticed her hairstyle.

Children's toys and activities, such as blowing bubbles; playing with Play-Doh, clay, or goop; coloring pictures; or drawing can be an amusing diversion for adults, too. Today's marketplace has a plethora of silly, technological gadgets for kids (and adults) that could make you laugh. What about a singing Christmas wreath, a chirping frog, or a small black ball that laughs a ridiculous laugh?

One year around Easter my dad visited a family friend who was at home dying of cancer. He handed her a fluffy yellow chick. She smiled as the little toy sang, "Peep, peep" in her hands. When she died several weeks later, she was buried with the little chick.

Humor is important. Some of these ideas may sound silly or weird, but give them a try!

Avoid the "A Positive Attitude Fixes Anything" Trap

Have you ever been told, "Just keep a positive attitude and everything will be fine"? There is no scientific or medical proof that a positive attitude will cure anyone of anything.

> *Here it was. <u>Cancer.</u> The dread disease and all that strength and self-sufficiency and health—cancelled. I was stripped of all that I had protected myself with. At the same time, doctors came with another "encouragement." "Your condition can best be helped if you have a positive attitude," they said. "A positive attitude!" I thought, "How can I have a positive attitude when I am probably going to die young. I won't have the time to enjoy the things I have worked for, and I will never get to see my daughter graduate or meet any of my grandchildren. Also, I am facing some length of time under chemotherapy with no assurance that it will even help my cancer. I should have a positive attitude when everything is wrong in what's left of my life?"*

Nevertheless, having a positive attitude *will* affect you. "It will improve your quality of life, no matter where you are in life or what you're having to go through," says social worker Nancy E. Weissman. "But, it's legitimate to have negative feelings about your illness—and it's much more important to allow yourself to feel emotions, such as sadness, fear and anger, than to hold them in."[12]

> *Be careful about telling them to keep a positive attitude. The health professionals like to use this lever to "encourage" their patients. It angered me. Besides, I found that it is not possible to come to a positive attitude until you come to terms with your disease. A positive*

attitude must be based on some sort of hope. If you are
hopeless, how can you work up a positive attitude?

Wendy Schlessel Harpham comments on those who promote this way of thinking: "They leave you with the impression that if you do not learn to manage all your stress and if you do not always have an optimistic outlook, then you are hurting your chances for improvement or cure. This approach leads to guilt and more stress." She also says that although self-help books can be very helpful for some people, their well-intentioned advice causes problems for others. "If the person dismisses the advice because he or she does not believe in it," Harpham says, "there may be some guilt about not doing 'everything possible.'"[13]

It's good to have a positive attitude as opposed to a nega-
tive attitude, but don't think that positive thinking will
buy you everything you want. The kind of positive think-
ing we should have is acceptance of the place we are in
because God has chosen that place for you and He
knows what is best for you.

Try to Keep Things "Normal"

When you spend hours, days, and even weeks at a time in clinics, doctors' offices, hospitals, or even your own home, you may feel overwhelmed by the gigantic task of getting better or stalling the progression of a disease. Being sick or disabled can really become a full-time job. This "job" can run your routine. How can you feel "normal" when your house looks like an overflowing warehouse for medical supplies or when your body doesn't act or respond the way it did in the past? Everything around you reminds you of your illness.

Your physician might also have given you strict rules and guidelines in order to maximize the benefits of your treatments or protect you from further side effects. My mom was unable to eat fresh fruit and vegetables or have fresh cut flowers or even a live Christmas tree before, during, and after any of her chemotherapy treatments. In other words, she had to think about her diet and her environment all of the time.

According to Haffey, you should keep as much of a routine as possible because it is an effective coping method. "Your goal in maintaining routines, both from the patient's perspective as well as that of the family members, is to keep things familiar. This sense of normalcy will help you ride the up and down ride that serious illness takes you on." It will also help you avoid the trap of overdoing it on good days.

Maintaining a routine includes returning to work, if at all possible, and keeping family traditions. Glenn Kirkland worked hard to maintain a social life. "I took Grace with me wherever I went: grocery shopping, walking on the canal, Alzheimer's disease meetings, as well as church," says Kirkland. "I tried to keep her physically, socially, emotionally, and spiritually active as much as practical."

A word of caution to family members: You need to be careful not to start treating your loved one differently just because he is ill. You play an important role in helping your loved one feel normal. Don't take away all his independence by doing everything for him. Don't treat him as if he cannot do anything anymore. Allow him to remain an active family member by participating in household responsibilities and making his own decisions.

Raymer advises family members to remind themselves that "no matter how sick someone is, he is still the same person as before." One way to alleviate any confusion in this area is for family members to ask, "How do you want me to help? Would you like me to do this or that?" Giving choices is always preferable.

Here are several specific suggestions to help foster an atmosphere of "normalcy" in your home:

- Continue to eat, sleep, and exercise regularly.
- Return to work (whatever that work may be) or pursue useful activities.
- Keep socializing with friends and family.
- Strike a balance, as best as you can, between a focus on the outside world and preparation for future problems.
- Continue to buy presents and new clothes for your loved one.
- Include your loved one in family chores and decisions.
- Go to movies, out to dinner, or take trips and vacations.
- Continue with physical intimacy, including cuddling and touching.
- Celebrate family holidays or birthdays as usual and do not postpone them.

Read the Bible and Pray

More than anything else, prayer and Bible reading will keep you and your family afloat during your crisis. Think of prayer as the glue that keeps your life together and your Bible as the framework that holds it all in place.

> *It is not the chemicals which have given me life this year, but the ministrations of the Spirit of God, which have enlivened me.*

In *Also My Journey*, Marguerite Atkins describes how she struggled to care for her husband. After fourteen years, she was sadder than ever, lonely, and not sure she wanted to go on. Then she cried out to God to help her. "It did not mean that the loneliness was gone, nor the restlessness at the life I was forced to live. It did not mean that the pain of watching Dick's increasing helplessness grew less. But it did mean that the despair that had been wrapping itself so slowly and relentlessly about me completely disappeared. I knew that it was God who had mercifully delivered me. And for that, I was deeply thankful."[14]

Even if you are having a hard time praying, you don't have to worry. The apostle Paul said that the Holy Spirit helps your weakness: "For we do not know how to pray as we should, but the Spirit Himself intercedes for us with groanings too deep for words" (Romans 8:26). What a comforting thought!

Virginia M. Anderson helped care for her two young nieces when her sister was diagnosed with ovarian cancer, and she herself has since been diagnosed with cancer. She explains what prayer does for her in the midst of trying circumstances: "I feel God's love washes over me in waves."

Can you describe the effect prayer has had on you in the past? How do you think prayer will work in your life right now?

Today, another setback. After feeling so good yesterday, today was not so good. Had my blood tested again and my white cell count is now below 500. Late afternoon I was running a slight fever. Dave and I prayed and by 8:30 p.m. I was improving. I can't help [but] believe that it was the Lord. My life, my only hope lives with Him.

Nancy J. Nordenson suggests several ways that you might pray when you have limited physical and emotional strength:

- Find a prayerful place (someplace quiet or out in nature).
- Use others' words (in the Bible, prayer books, or hymns).
- Meditate on Jesus' life (He felt pain, too).
- Assume a posture of prayer, such as kneeling or lying face down.
- Write out your prayers.

- Pray with your tears.
- Ask others to pray for you.[15]

Throughout the course of my struggles, my Bible was ever beside me. I read as a starving person reaches for food. With each drought, I found sustenance and new hope began to build.

Painful circumstances are often the driving force behind prayer. Read through the Psalms and notice how often the psalmists cry out to God in the midst of their suffering. They claim God's faithfulness even in their fear, anger, and sadness. They kept praying despite what was happening to them and what they were feeling. I basically lived in the Psalms throughout the entire length of my mom's illness.

I turned to the Bible for help and comfort. Since I had so little energy many days were spent just lying on a couch. Often I would turn to the Psalms and there I found that the Psalmists had much the same pain in their situations as I had and as they cried to God for help, I found a voice to do similarly.

F

FEED ON THE WORD

Meditating on biblical passages that show God's love and mercy will strengthen and encourage both patients and caregivers. Consider memorizing the following Scriptures.

- The LORD is my light and my salvation; whom shall I fear? The LORD is the defense of my life; whom shall I dread?… For in the day of trouble He will conceal me in His tabernacle; in the secret place of His tent He will hide me; He will lift me up on a rock. (Psalm 27:1, 5)

- I would have despaired unless I had believed that I would see the goodness of the LORD in the land of the living. Wait for the LORD; be strong, and let your heart take courage; yes, wait for the LORD. (Psalm 27:13–14)
- For His anger is but for a moment, His favor is for a lifetime; weeping may last a night, but a shout of joy comes in the morning. (Psalm 30:5)
- Because Thy lovingkindness is better than life, my lips shall praise Thee.... When I remember Thee on my bed, I meditate on Thee in the night watches, for Thou hast been my help, and in the shadow of Thy wings I sing for joy. My soul clings to Thee; Thy right hand upholds me. (Psalm 63:3, 6–8)
- For Thou, Lord, art good, and ready to forgive, and abundant in lovingkindness to all who call upon Thee.... In the day of my trouble I shall call upon Thee, for Thou wilt answer me. (Psalm 86:5, 7)
- For as high as the heavens are above the earth, so great is His lovingkindness toward those who fear Him.... Just as a father has compassion on his children, so the LORD has compassion on those who fear Him. (Psalm 103:11, 13)
- Then they cried out to the LORD in their trouble; He delivered them from their distress. (Psalm 107:6)
- He has made His wonders to be remembered; the LORD is gracious and compassionate. (Psalm 111:4)
- The LORD is good to all, and His mercies are over all His works. (Psalm 145:9)
- The LORD's lovingkindnesses indeed never cease, for His compassions never fail. They are new every morning; great is Thy faithfulness.... The LORD is good to those who wait for Him, to the person who seeks Him. (Lamentations 3:22–23, 25)
- Finally, brethren, rejoice, be made complete, be comforted, be

like-minded, live in peace; and the God of love and peace shall be with you. (2 Corinthians 13:11)

- Now may our Lord Jesus Christ Himself and God our Father, who has loved us and given us eternal comfort and good hope by grace, comfort and strengthen your hearts in every good work and word. (2 Thessalonians 2:16–17)

- Draw near to God and He will draw near to you. (James 4:8)

The mind of man plans his way,
But the LORD directs his steps.

PROVERBS 16:9

———◆◆◆———

F
I have one life and one chance to make it count for something…
I'm free to choose what that something is, and
the something I've chosen is my faith.
Now, my faith goes beyond theology and religion and
requires considerable work and effort.
My faith demands—this is not optional—my faith demands
that I do whatever I can,
wherever I am,
whenever I can,
for as long as I can with whatever I have to try to make a difference.

JIMMY CARTER

SIX

The Highest Priority

I sat in the chair facing my boss's desk and waited. The door closed—a little too loudly—and he walked around to his side of the desk. "Have you decided to work full-time for us?" he asked immediately.

"I'd like to continue to work part-time until after my mom's chemotherapy treatments are finished," I replied without hesitation. I glanced at his face, trying to read his expression. "Her treatments will last six months," I added.

"Well…if that's what you've decided," he said, "but I can't promise the position will still be open in September."

"Thanks for understanding," I said as I headed back to my desk. I glanced out the window at the tarmac of Boston's Logan International Airport. Another plane was ready for takeoff. As it roared down the runway, I tried to focus on the piles of projects stacked everywhere. *Just pick one and get started,* I told myself, but questions formed in my mind. *Did I make the right choice? Did he really understand or care? Will there be another position available for me when I want it? Are we going to have enough money to last through this summer of long-distance phone calls and weekend trips to Maryland?*

It only took a few minutes to remind myself, again, that what was really at stake was spending time with my mom. I didn't want to miss helping and encouraging her through a very difficult experience. She was much more important than a job and a few extra dollars.

I have never regretted my decision to work part-time during those first few months of my mom's illness. Later, as we wrestled with our priorities in the light of Mom's illness, Steve and I had to make other decisions about our finances, our schedule, and even our geographic location. In this chapter, you'll discover how setting priorities for your time and energy can help bring peace to both patients and caregivers.

IDENTIFY YOUR VALUES

Before you can set priorities, you need to be clear about what you value. Mary Raymer highly recommends writing down what is important to you. She says that listing your values will help you realize that "they are still your principles for life, regardless of your health situation."

Read through the following list of values. To focus your thoughts, you might want to write out an example or explanation next to the values that are most important to you. When you have finished, follow the steps to find your "top ten" core values.[1]

Character Values

> ethical with money
> faithful
> honest
> teachable
> loving
> loyal
> morally pure
> obedient
> patient
> temperate
> tolerant
> trustworthy
> truthful

Civic and Cultural Values

- committed to specific issues
- law-abiding
- patriotic
- socially responsible

Personal Development Values

- cleanly
- developing skills and hobbies
- disciplined
- growing intellectually
- living according to personal health convictions

Relational Values

- caring
- compassionate
- friendly
- generous
- giving
- gracious
- helpful
- kind
- merciful
- respectful of others
- serving
- thoughtful

Moral Values

- committed to certain moral precepts
- taking stands on certain moral issues

Lifestyle Values

    adhering to a work ethic
    emphasizing material things
    emphasizing relationships
    managing my time

Family Values

    committed to my mate
    committed to family members
    committed to grandparents and relatives

Spiritual Values

    being full of hope
    being submissive
    being tenderhearted
    depending upon God
    fearing (revering) God
    forgiving
    having a contrite heart
    having a childlike faith
    hungering after righteousness
    loving God with a whole heart
    praying humbly
    serving God
    trusting Christ as Savior and Lord
    trusting the Bible
    viewing life according to God's agenda

Other Values

_____

_____

_____

Now put an asterisk by the twenty values that you think are most essential in your life. Next, narrow the list to ten, and rank the values in order of importance.

My Top Ten Values

1. _____

2. _____

3. _____

4. _____

5. _____

6. _____

7. _____

8. _____

9. _____

10. _____

Finally, reflect on your lifestyle and what you do with your time. How well do your activities reflect your core values? Do you really live according to your values? You may want to look at a calendar or ask a family member to help you determine this. Think of several examples of activities that either do or don't reflect your values. It's important to analyze which values certain activities represent. This will help you discover what you truly value.

For example, if you chose *committed to grandparents and relatives* as a core value, ask yourself how often you visited them in the past year. If distance made that difficult, ask yourself how often you called or wrote to them. If this is truly one of your core values, identify changes you could make in your lifestyle that would permit you to live it out more fully.

> *There is a difference in what we say we believe and in what we actually believe. The only way is to check how we actually live. I had determined to follow Jesus twenty-five years ago and had, since that time, studied and tried to apply the principles I learned from the Bible. But something was missing. Try as I would to practice what I read, there were areas which simply did not conform. I was too caught up in materialism, for example, and without realizing it, my goals became things or trips that I found fascinating rather than God's work in me to perfect me and prepare me for life eternal.*

Choose Your Activities

You may be wondering how your life can possibly reflect all the values you embraced before your illness. True, it may be necessary for you to figure out a new way to live out the values of_____
_____because you can no longer
_____ (You fill in the blank.)

My mom valued service and spent much of her time doing things for other people. During her illness, she was often the one being served, which left her feeling frustrated and unhappy. But she trusted God for the grace and humility to accept this and incorporated generous acts of service in her daily life as long as she was able. Her gifts of love ranged from preparing home-cooked gourmet meals (which she would sometimes start before leaving for an outpatient medical procedure), mending a favorite shirt, or writing a lengthy letter to encourage a friend. She gained satisfaction from staying true to one of her core values.

You may not be able to live out your values in the same way that you did before, but you can find new and different ways to do so. Most likely, you will have to choose which activities are most important in light of your values. Taking a few minutes to set your priorities will help you feel more in control of your schedule.

Despite physical or other limitations, you should still try to incorporate the activities you identify as priorities into your daily, weekly, or monthly schedule. The following ideas will help you make the most of your time and energy.

As a patient, you can:

- Share your list of goals and priorities with your family so that they can support your efforts.
- Make your own decisions about your health, schedule, and activities.
- Fill odd and unpredictable moments. Keep a book, a writing pad, or note cards with you at all times. If you find yourself stuck waiting somewhere, you'll be able to use those precious moments.
- Keep your calendar with you so that you can keep track of doctor's appointments without having to call the office later.
- Take over any chores you are physically or mentally able to handle and turn over any you cannot. For example, if you were previously in charge of mowing the lawn, now you may want to switch to balancing the checkbook.
- Pace yourself. (Read chapter 5 again if necessary.)
- Maintain a regular routine.
- Keep lists to stay as organized as possible.
- Decide who you want your visitors to be. Let's face it: Some people are draining to be around. If you have limited energy, have a family member screen visitors.
- Concentrate on accomplishing only one small goal each day, week, or month; and then feel really good about what you did.

- Focus on your priorities. Ask yourself: If I am interrupted while doing something important, which parts of it do I want to make sure get done?[2]
- Let unimportant tasks and duties stay undone, or encourage a family member to do them.

As a family member or close friend, you can:

- Emotionally and physically support your loved one as he pursues his goals.
- Help set up a visitation schedule that makes it clear when people can visit and how long they can stay. If someone overstays his welcome, help that well-meaning but insensitive person to leave. You could designate one family member as the boundary keeper and devise nonverbal cues to signal when it is time for a visitor to go.
- Strengthen your loved one whenever he is working on a strenuous project for work, a ministry, or a hobby. You can take phone messages, put a note on the front door to discourage visitors, provide snacks and drinks, keep household noise down—anything that will help protect this block of time and make it as productive as possible for your loved one.
- Do extra work around the house (only if this will not cause your loved one unnecessary stress). If you think this will offend him, consider offering your help first.
- Help create an environment in which your loved one is doing at least some of the work.
- Be available, but don't hover.
- Lower your own expectations of what will get done in order to reduce stress on yourself, your family, and your loved one.

- Make allowances in everybody's schedule for recovery time. You will need to help your loved one set aside this critically needed downtime.
- Find timesavers for yourself and your household.
- Write things down.
- Plan your errands carefully. Run them at times when there isn't much traffic.
- Make a list beforehand and map out a route.

I am beginning to place my priorities differently than before. Since there is so little energy, each day has to be carefully thought through so as to have energy for those things which are of the highest priority. Often, only essential activities such as preparing food or going to work can be accomplished. I no longer have energy for simple things, such as talking on the phone to a friend.

ENJOY EACH MOMENT

While identifying values, setting priorities, and choosing activities can relieve stress and produce satisfaction, being content is paramount. What is contentment? Jeremiah Burroughs, a puritan preacher and reformer in seventeenth-century England, defined it as "the sweet, inward, quiet, gracious frame of spirit, which freely submits to and delights in God's wise and fatherly disposal in every condition."[3]

Still no direction for the future. There is something, though, which surprises me. I don't know when I first noticed it, but it was sometime during my recuperation—a bubbling, exuberant joy that I cannot explain. Sometimes I just feel overwhelmed by this feeling of joy. I know it is from the Lord for I feel it when there is not necessarily anything I should feel happy about.

Becoming content is a learned process. The apostle Paul said that he *learned* to be content in whatever circumstances he was in. "I know how to get along with humble means, and I also know how to live in prosperity; in any and every circumstance I have learned the secret of being filled and going hungry, both of having abundance and suffering need" (Philippians 4:11–12). Paul's claim is amazing when you consider what he went through: severe beatings, imprisonment, persecution, hunger, and exposure to dangerous natural elements, including a shipwreck (see 2 Corinthians 11:23–33 and Acts 27:14–44).

Joni Eareckson Tada agrees that contentment doesn't just happen, especially when we're in circumstances beyond our control. In fact, she says, contentment is an education, a kind of schooling, which requires you to make tough choices. "Although contentment is a direct result of the application of God's grace in our lives, we only arrive at it through a learned discipline. A discipline of choosing not to resist God in spite of difficult circumstances. A discipline of choosing to believe."[4]

If I only sit back and analyze what has occurred in my life, I know that I have been blessed in many ways. I must learn to let go of the dream of enjoying life in the future and learn to enjoy it now.

How did Paul learn to be content in his circumstances? How can you learn to be content in yours? In Philippians 4, Paul points out the three spiritual resources that make contentment possible. The first is the overruling providence of God (v. 10). When you realize that God is in control of your life and its seemingly out-of-control events, you have a basis for true contentment. The second is the unfailing power of God (vv. 11–13). His power knows no limits, and it can work in you to give you the contentment you desire. The third is the unchanging promise of God (vv. 14–20). He has promised to take care of your needs (see Matthew 5:25–34).[5]

We need to choose to discipline our attitudes toward external circumstances, confident that God will give us the grace and strength necessary for each day, one moment at a time (see 2 Corinthians 12:9–10; Philippians 4:13; 1 Peter 5:5; Hebrews 12:15).

If you find yourself feeling discontented, check your thought life. Are you constantly concentrating on all the worst aspects of your situation? Do you rehearse potential disasters in your mind? You can indulge yourself in this area every once in a while, but be careful—it can quickly become a habit. Paul would advise you to protect your thought life. Keep thinking good things and then act on them. (Read Philippians 4:8–9 again.)

Today, I received word that my CA-125 is on the rise. For one year I have expected it—now it is a reality. It may be a misreading, and I have no desire to worry Dave before I know the truth…but I don't know if I can keep it from him. It is a further step in trust. I must learn to control my imagination to allow Jesus to fill my thoughts when I am tempted to dwell on the what ifs.

And remember, says Tada, "God doesn't expect you to handle the burden of next week, the cross of next year. Whether you are in a prison, a hospital, an office, or in your home, by God's grace, contentment is yours today."[6]

Tonight at the Ash Wednesday service the Lord revealed something to me that made a lot of sense. I have been trying to think about how I would handle death should it be in the not-too-distant future for me. The Lord revealed to me that I have not resolved that thought because I have not needed to. He will give me grace to accept that also when the time comes. He has given me the grace to accept everything else so far. Praise Him!

EMBRACE GOD'S PLAN FOR YOU

Living life with purpose and meaning is another major component of being content in your circumstances. If you stop to look at the bigger picture of life and discover how each day can be and is, in fact, part of that larger plan, you will feel less tension. You do not have to be physically healthy to live with purpose.

My goal is to really know God—to know His character, to seek His will as I have never sought it before. It is no simple thing I endeavor, for I desire to walk within His kingdom. No more of the paltry, earthly goals. There is so much more and occasionally, like today, I get a clouded glimpse of that great glory just beyond my sight. It somehow has something to do with asking God for great things, and asking for my temporal life to be extended seems too small a thing to even consider. It is just not important in this new vision.

Read through these Bible verses, which speak of our purpose here on earth. This is not an exhaustive list, so feel free to look up others on your own.

- What does the LORD require of you but to do justice, to love kindness, and to walk humbly with your God? (Micah 6:8)
- Whether, then, you eat or drink or whatever you do, do all to the glory of God. (1 Corinthians 10:31)
- Therefore we also have as our ambition, whether at home or absent, to be pleasing to Him. (2 Corinthians 5:9)

- He died for all, that they who live should no longer live for themselves, but for Him who died and rose again on their behalf. (2 Corinthians 5:15)
- To the end that we who were the first to hope in Christ should be to the praise of His glory. (Ephesians 1:12)
- For we are His workmanship, created in Christ Jesus for good works, which God prepared beforehand, that we should walk in them. (Ephesians 2:10)
- More than that, I count all things to be loss in view of the surpassing value of knowing Christ Jesus my Lord. (Philippians 3:8)
- I press on toward the goal for the prize of the upward call of God in Christ Jesus. (Philippians 3:14)
- Bodily discipline is only of little profit, but godliness is profitable for all things, since it holds the promise for the present life and also for the life to come.... For it is this we labor and strive, because we have fixed our hope on the living God, who is the Savior of all men, especially of believers. (1 Timothy 4:8, 10)
- [Christ Jesus] gave Himself for us, that He might redeem us from every lawless deed and purify for Himself a people for His own possession, zealous for good deeds. (Titus 2:14)

What do you believe are some of your purposes here on earth? One of my primary purposes in life is_____

_____

Another purpose for living is _____

_____

Do you think that concentrating on your purpose will help you be more content with your physical situation? If so, how? If not, why not? _____

_____

_____

The quiet click of the knitting needles produces a rhythm for my reveries. Outside the trees are bending over under the ice, which came in the night, creating a white, cold yet beautiful backdrop. It reminds me that my own winter came quickly, while I would have been considered in the prime of life. It happens that way sometimes. It is neither good nor bad; it just is.

We are all born with great promise. Within each tiny life is the potential for a successful life. But we are all born with the wrong idea of what success is. Therein lies the dilemma. We think that success is feeding our desires, but that is the failure of the greatest sort. Most of the time it takes a lifetime to realize the fallacy of our thinking. The hope is that we will realize it before we come to the end.

As I approach my own final breath, I find that I have a desire to leave with the world the wisdom that my lifetime has produced. Even though mine was short, suffering has caused a shortening of the learning curve. I speak as one who has come from the furnace and can only hope that my voice might at least prepare someone else for their own fire. I am totally convinced that none of us leave this world without having to walk through the purging flames at some time in their life.

Some go through this time and call it hell and learn little. This is unfortunate, for such a time is there in order for us to approach heaven. It is only as we see it as a time to realize the purpose of our lives that we will finally approach death having learned all that we were meant to learn.

Before my own time of pain, I was a much more self-centered person. I thought that I was here to enjoy life. Although there is some truth in that, it is not the total purpose of life. It was the same idea that the baby has as he enters the world: my desires are to be fed so that I will be happy.

There are many people who never go beyond this. I could have been one of those, but sickness intervened. Suddenly, I was forced to cross the line from the haves to the have-nots. I no longer had my health and as a result, I no longer had control over my life.

How easy it is to be deluded into thinking that the life will be rewarded with temporal pleasures. Now that I analyze it, I can't think of why I held that position. I certainly did lip service to the fact that the most important things in life were not earthly pleasures, but when I did my planning for the future, I lived to enjoy those things. What is worse, when I became ill, I felt like I was punished because it was the earthly pleasures that I was regretting giving up.

As the weeks went by, I read the Psalms and found a wealth of proper attitudes. Surely the psalmists had experienced much of the same loss of earthly safety, but they found even greater blessings in the God who gives life to all. I began to find real life.

In the end, I lost my life. That life is gone forever, and I am relieved to be rid of it. In its place, I have a new life. In this one, I have found real freedom—freedom from fear, freedom from worry, freedom from materialism. Of course I am not perfect and if I wander too far from the Lord, I will revert back to my past struggles. It is a warning.

I began to understand the verse "I am crucified with Christ and it is no longer I who live, but Christ lives in me and the life that I now live, I live by faith in the Son of God who loves me and delivered Himself up for me." In dying to self, we finally learn to live.

Most of us are unaware of the heavenly agenda behind each event in our lives. We see ourselves in charge. But look behind the scenes and you will see the hand of God, bringing about challenges, which test us and give us an opportunity to live for something more important than material things or temporary fame. The ultimate goal for God is to create His life in us, for only then will we find the peace and joy we seek and only then will we be prepared for the life which follows this one.

F

IDENTIFYING VALUES, SCHEDULING ACTIVITIES, AND SETTING GOALS

This evaluation section can help you mesh your values, activities, priorities, and goals so you can feel more comfortable with your new lifestyle. These crucial decisions can reduce stress for you and your family. As you work through this section, keep in mind what you've just learned about contentment and purpose in life.

Values and Activities

YOUR TOP TEN VALUES	CURRENT ACTIVITIES	MODIFIED ACTIVITIES
1. _____	_____	_____
2. _____	_____	_____
3. _____	_____	_____
4. _____	_____	_____

5. _____   _____   _____

6. _____   _____   _____

7. _____   _____   _____

8. _____   _____   _____

9. _____   _____   _____

10. _____   _____   _____

If you had to pick only three of these activities to act upon per day, week, or month, which would they be? Which value is most important to you?

_____

_____

Priorities

Think back over the past month. How many activities did you participate in that did not correspond with your core values?

_____

_____

_____

_____

Which of these activities do you still want to pursue?

_____

_____

_____

_____

Which activities can you drop from your schedule?

_____

_____

_____

_____

_____

You may want to make a list of all your pursuits during a day or a week to help you evaluate your priorities. Once you have made that list, number each entry in order of its importance to you.

DAILY ACTIVITIES   WEEKLY ACTIVITIES

_____   _____

_____   _____

_____   _____

_____   _____

_____   _____

_____   _____

_____   _____

_____   _____

_____   _____

_____   _____

Goals

According to Rev. Bruce D. Johnson, goals are *Godly Objectives Assuring Lasting Success.*[7] Learning how to set goals (allowing for delays and changes) can help you be content with your accomplishments despite limitations of time and energy.

Consider the following eight key areas of life:

1. spiritual   _____

_____

2. intellectual _____

_____

3. physical   _____

_____

4. family   _____

_____

5. professional _____

_____

6. financial   _____

_____

7. relational   _____

_____

8. personal   _____

_____

Spend some time dreaming about what you would like to see in each of these areas of your life. You can do this on your own or with your spouse, a family member, or close friend. Then put your list away for at least a week or two, but continue to think about your dreams.

Now you're ready to set goals to help you realize your most important dreams. "Goals need to be creative, difficult [to help inspire us to change], congruent, balanced, and flexible," says Johnson. "Also, putting a time limit or deadline on reaching them can help you stay focused until you accomplish them." Keep in mind that good goals are SMART goals:

S – spiritually driven

M – measurable (or specific)

A – achievable

R – reaching

T – timed

GOALS	PLANS OR SPECIFIC STEPS	NEEDED BY WHEN?
Short-Term		
Intermediate-term		
Long-term		

Two are better than one because
they have a good return for their labor.
For if either of them falls,
the one will lift up his companion.
But woe to the one who falls
when there is not another to lift him.

ECCLESIASTES 4:9–10

———◆◆———

F
'Tis the human touch in this world that counts,
The touch of your hand in mine,
Which means far more to the fainting heart
Than shelter and bread and wine;
For shelter is gone when the night is o'er,
And bread lasts only a day,
But the touch of the hand and the sound of a voice
Sing on in the soul alway.

SPENCER MICHAEL FREE

Seven

The Touch
of Your Hand

I boarded the plane without any magazines in my carry-on bag. How could I read anything? I peered past droplets of icy rain dripping down the tiny window and stared at the bleakness. As the plane sped down the runway and thrust itself into the grey sky, waves of panic washed over my mind. *What would she look like? What could I say to encourage her? How should I act?* These thoughts assailed me the entire flight.

Rebecca was at the gate waiting for me, and we went immediately to the hospital, exchanging only a few words on the way. When I stepped out of the elevator, the many smells of a hospital assaulted my nose, making me feel nauseous and light-headed. Finally, I reached Mom's room.

Peeking around the door, I saw her for the first time since her surgery. Her back was to me, and she was trying in vain to get something out of one of her bags. She looked so thin! At that point, I must have made a noise, because she turned around. I just stood there. Again, I felt a sense of panic, wondering what I should do or say.

"Hi, Mom," I said hesitantly, almost as if it were a question.

"How was your flight?" she asked.

"Fine."

A huge cloud of awkwardness enveloped us. Everything about life, her health, and our relationship was different; and I didn't know how to act. I felt confused. *Should I ask her how she feels?* I asked myself. Finally, I did what I had wanted to do all along—I walked to her bedside and hugged her for a long time.

Over the days, weeks, and months that followed, I learned that I didn't need to treat my mom any differently than before because all she wanted from me was me. I realized how much she needed her family and friends to support her. None of us want to face difficult times alone.

Loving support from people who care is essential for anyone coping with a serious illness. Its value is truly immeasurable. Each one of us—as a spouse, family member, pastor or lay minister, fellow church member, close friend, acquaintance, coworker, or neighbor—can make a concrete difference through our presence, words, and actions. Whether we realize it or not, we can help a loved one deal better with a serious illness.

LETTING OTHERS HELP

As a patient, the most important thing you can do for your loved one is to let him help you. If at first you feel too proud, uncomfortable, depressed, fearful, or embarrassed to ask—or even let—someone help you, remember that it's okay to feel that way. Acknowledge how hard it is to watch others do things for you that you've always been able to manage yourself. It's tough to let go of control, and if you're really struggling with this, you may want to reread chapter 2 to remind yourself that God is in control and with you every step of the way.

This is not an easy road to travel. Yesterday I came in for what was supposed to be a quick procedure, a new groshong. Not so—a small puncture in my lung, and I was in serious pain. That meant a night in the hospital— a night of misery. The Lord told me something in the process. I was feeling very strongly about taking care of myself—not wanting to put anyone out. I was determined to drive myself to the various appointments. The result was both Dave and Becky came down last night, and I had to accept it. Becky will have to come back to pick me up.

You have too much to gain from allowing others to pitch in where needed to let those emotional barriers remain in place. Wendy Schlessel Harpham points out three main advantages for the patient who accepts help:

- You can devote your time and energy to taking care of your medical needs and the decisions you need to make.
- You can get more rest if you want or need it.
- You will have more time to communicate with your family and friends, create a supportive network, and work through some of your feelings.[1]

A publication of the National Cancer Institute says that although choosing to help friends by telling them what you need is not easy and takes energy you may feel you don't have, the rewards can be exhilarating. "We all feel better giving than receiving, so it might be easier if you think of your requests for assistance as letting others feel useful, rather than as petitions for help."[2]

PASTORAL CARE

Instead of resisting help, you may feel overwhelmed and in need of a greater support system than you have. As a patient you can help yourself by seeking outside professional support. No one who is trying to cope with chronic or serious illness should ever overlook emotional and spiritual assistance. Over and over again in her journal, Mom mentions a pastor or lay minister who came over to talk and pray with her.

> *Dr. Kinloch came over this noon, and we had a good conversation. Talked about how we are to live in God's mansions—same root word as abiding. Compare Psalm 90 and 91 with John 15.*

Pastors, chaplains, lay ministers, and other spiritual leaders are in a privileged position to offer special care to hurting people. Oftentimes, people view pastors and chaplains as the tangible presence of God and are spiritually hungry for whatever they can offer, particularly during a crisis. "Pastors can provide peace and perspective," says Dr. Gregg Seckman. "Times of crisis are windows of opportunity when people are especially thirsty for spiritual nourishment. A pastor cannot let them pass by."[3]

Dr. Marlin C. Hardman stresses the importance of biblically based pastoral guidance in helping hurting people. "Apart from the truth of Scripture, we frequently misinterpret our circumstances," he says. "People need to feel the support of genuine interest in them and know that others are remembering them specifically in prayer." Another aspect of pastoral guidance is having people confide in you when they may not be able to confide in another family member or friend, adds Hardman.[4]

Rev. Robert Steinke believes that the love chapter in 1 Corinthians 13 is an applicable guide for all those supporting and caring for someone who is seriously ill:

> Love is patient, love is kind, and is not jealous; love does not brag and is not arrogant, does not act unbecomingly; it does not seek its own, is not provoked, does not take into account a wrong suffered, does not rejoice in unrighteous-

ness, but rejoices with the truth; bears all things, believes all things, hopes all things, endures all things. (vv. 4–7)

"When you can provide someone with a truly loving presence in the midst of the hard situation," Steinke says, "it will help them remain more patient and more hopeful. You can be like a visible presence of God—Him shining through you."

Rev. Joseph Nilsen believes that his physical presence with individuals and their families is the most important part of his supportive role as a chaplain. He refers to it as a "ministry of presence" and says that frequent, brief visits are key. He also tries to connect the family to sources of practical help and support.[5]

The most important thing for Rev. Faye Serene is to understand where patients are so that she can really be there for them. "I want to take the time and allow the space for grieving, anger, bargaining, denial, or acceptance," she says, "so the person and family have the opportunity to express their emotions—whatever those emotions are."[6]

What are some specific ways pastors, chaplains, lay ministers, and other spiritual leaders can effectively communicate their care and concern for those facing a serious illness? Pastors and chaplains with many years of experience of working with the seriously ill suggest the following:[7]

- Be a good listener. Ask him how he is doing.
- Be with him.
- Focus on the person. (Do not share your own personal stories.)
- Be a good sounding board by acknowledging the validity of what he is going through or feeling.
- Be comfortable sitting in silence. (If at times you're not sure what to say, it's better not to say anything.)
- Be sensitive to any concerns the patient or family may have,

including fear of the manner of death, hope of resurrection, unfinished relational issues or other conflicts, funeral concerns, and a family member trying to do all the care alone.

- Recognize that the mate and family are anxious and under great stress.
- Pray with them and for them.
- Share Bible verses. (Exercise caution here. Make sure you've listened to his needs first.)
- Create an environment where the patient can feel comfortable sharing openly and honestly.
- Think about what you're doing and your motives for doing it.
- Start developing your library, resources, and skills in this area and allow God to help teach you.

It may seem as if there are a lot of things to remember when visiting someone who is seriously ill, but according to Rev. Robert Grohman, the most important is to be open to God's guidance. "I simply try to be a comforting presence. I don't come in with a set game plan, so I can be sensitive to God and do whatever He is leading me to do in a particular situation," he says.[8]

Even though there are many things that a pastoral visitor can do and say to show his care for and genuine interest in an individual and his family, there are also some potential pitfalls. Based on advice from experienced pastors and chaplains, the following list describes what a spiritual leader should refrain from doing when giving pastoral care to a seriously ill individual:[9]

- Do not assume anything about anyone you are visiting.
- Do not visit without calling first.
- Do not come in with your own agenda and things you want to see accomplished.
- Do not say "I understand what you're going through" or "I know how you feel."

- Do not neglect any family member.
- Do not be quick to judge others who are in pain. (You don't want to condemn him for his thinking as he tries to express the intensity of his feelings.)
- Do not make promises you cannot keep. Don't say, "Everything is going to be fine."
- Only say what you know is true—true of yourself, true of the person, and true of God.
- Do not overstay your welcome. Be sensitive about when you should leave. (Shorter, frequent visits are usually better.)
- Do not discuss personal family business, including wills and bequests unless you are specifically asked.
- Do not breach confidentiality. (Keep in mind that sometimes when people are hurting, they say things that they ordinarily wouldn't. Never pass that information along to anyone.)
- Do not minister to people like a physician writes out a prescription. (For example, don't say, "Look, just trust the Lord; He'll work it out. Just read these few verses and you'll feel better.")

Pastoral care, whether through a church, hospital, or hospice organization, can be an invaluable encouragement to a patient and his family. Pastors, chaplains, and lay ministers should remember that it is not just *what* is done and said but *how* it is done and said that makes a big difference to people.

WHEN TWO ARE ONE

Genesis 2:24 says that "a man shall leave his father and his mother, and shall cleave to his wife; and they shall become one flesh." Becoming one within the confines of a marriage goes beyond the physical meaning of becoming one flesh. Ideally, there is an emotional and spiritual oneness that develops as two individuals come together over time. God intends that a couple complement each other, enjoy companionship, and mirror God's image (Genesis 1:26–27).

> *The week of treatment was especially tough since Dave was also gone. I missed his support.*

This kind of marriage relationship provides a deep level of support for both partners as they go through life helping and encouraging each other. Therefore, it is no surprise that when one spouse suffers, the other also experiences pain. If your spouse is seriously ill, you may be swirling around in a whirlwind of emotions as you try to help him. My dad says that it felt like "life stood still and we were in a never-never land." Absolutely everything revolved around supporting my mom. "I adjusted my work schedule from 7 A.M. to 4 P.M., cancelled or postponed business trips, and spent every evening and weekend with her," he adds.

As a spouse, you will probably carry the biggest burden of support, so it's crucial to remain emotionally connected and take time to reflect on the seriousness of your marriage vows—"for better or for worse…in sickness and in health." Supporting and staying connected to a seriously ill partner requires courage, faith, and commitment, but it also brings great rewards for both parties.

One of my dad's special memories is of the two of them sharing food he had smuggled in for dinner, when she was supposed to be dining on hospital fare. On the way to visit her, he would stop at a gourmet food store and pick up freshly made sandwiches and ice cream. After he sneaked the food upstairs to her room in the clinic, they would spend a few minutes in prayer before enjoying their meal. "We had some of our best conversations during those mealtimes," my dad remembers.

Dad believes that communication is one of the keys to enduring a health-care crisis. "We had always practiced open and honest communication, and this continued throughout the many years of her illness," he says. "This made the happy times happier and the sad times more bearable."

Keep in mind that during most prolonged illnesses, there will be moments, or even extended periods, of respite. Enjoy those to their fullest in whatever way you can. The up times can help both of you persevere through the down times.

Here we are in London. As we deplaned this morning, I discovered that my feet were swollen. Why do I immediately associate any problem with my cancer?... We took a three hour nap then had a light lunch and went for a sight-seeing tour starting at Piccadilly Circus and Trafalgar Square. We enjoyed it immensely. As we flew over, I was overwhelmed by the way the Lord has so abundantly blessed me. Who could have imagined that I should ever travel again?

There are many ways you can show your spouse how much you care.[10]

- Stay emotionally involved.
- Be realistic but positive. This will help leave open the doors of communication.
- Read the Bible together and pray often.
- Listen to music or sing songs together.
- Frequently ask, "What are you thinking about?" or "What would you like to talk about?"
- Listen, listen, listen.
- Help with decisions if asked, or make them together.
- Do as much as you possibly can—cook, clean house, etc.
- Laugh together.
- Cry together.
- Respect silence.

- Hug and hold each other often.
- Give lots of verbal affirmation—say "I love you" a lot.
- Cultivate an attitude of appreciation and gratitude for past times together.
- Continue to show affection that does not end up in a physical relationship. (There may come a time when you will no longer be able to have a sexual relationship. You need to accept that and keep things as normal as possible.)
- Realize that your privacy will most likely have some limitations with so many people coming and going.
- Drugs and other medical treatments may cause drastic emotional changes. Be as patient and forgiving as you possibly can.
- Address any worries the patient may have. Often he may be concerned about other family members and need your reassurance that they will be taken care of.

I fear that I have hurt Dave with my words last night. He who has only done his best for me and loved me unconditionally. I am so mean-spirited, it appalls me. How awful if I should leave him with the idea that he has not measured up to my standards when, in truth, he has exceeded all that I could have wished from him. Without Dave, my life would have been boring and I would have long since buried myself in my insecurities. Dave, how I love you! How I wish I could have been a better wife to you in my verbal support area. How I wish I did not have to leave you alone!

Another important way you can show your support is by dealing with any unresolved issues. Initiating discussion should be the primary responsibility of the healthy spouse. "In the last two or three months of my wife's illness, there were things that we needed to say to each other," says Dr. Marlin C. Hardman. "There were things that needed to be forgiven as well as things for which we needed to ask forgiveness." Gil Wesley remembers how he and his late wife, Debbie, decided to "go deep" in order to resolve all relational issues. "There is a huge pressure not to bring things up when someone is dying," says Wesley, "but I am so glad we did. At the very, very end we looked at each other and agreed that there were no regrets."

Be assured that if you give your spouse unconditional love and support throughout his time of need, he will receive strength, peace, and encouragement. Hardman will never forget the meaningful conversation he and his wife had approximately two months before her death. He remembers seeing her lying in bed, weak and vulnerable. She thanked him for hanging in there with her through everything. "It was then that I knew I had been a strengthening influence in her life, and I was so glad," says Hardman.

There are also extra benefits you will gain as a result of your giving and support. My dad believes that he gained a better appreciation for the simple things of life and learned to enjoy the here and now without counting on tomorrow. He says that now "the trick is to prioritize my time and efforts to make sure that I continue living this way." Hardman says that he has never been the same. "I am able to minister to hurting people now because I have earned the right to do and say certain things."

David, my beloved—it is you I most hate to leave. You alone could have stood me. You have loved me unconditionally and put up with so much. I love you forever.

FAMILY SUPPORT

Throughout my mom's illness, all I wanted to do was to help her—help ease her pain and discomfort, help prepare her food, help her laugh, and help encourage her. It made me feel better about the entire situation when I was actively helping her. I knew that Mom became frustrated as she struggled with a lack of independence as she lost control over her life. She needed us more and more, and it was upsetting to her. She also seemed to feel guilty about the burdens placed on us. I'll never forget our conversation during her last hospital stay, when she was feeling acute pangs of guilt and sadness.

"You don't have to be here, you know," she announced. After a short pause, she added, "This is too much to ask of you." She was referring to the decision my sister and I had made to become her primary caregivers once she came home under hospice care.

"Mom, where else would we be and what else would we do?" we asked. "We feel honored to have this opportunity to serve you. We cannot even begin to pay you back for all of the millions of things you have done for us our entire lives. We are so lucky to get this chance to help you."

Just as much as she needed us, we desperately needed her to let us help in any way that we could.

Another day spent at NIH, but this time with Becky. I hope she was able to study enough.

As a family member, you are in a wonderful position to offer your seriously ill loved one unconditional love and support.

The very best thing you can offer is your presence. According to Rosemary Elsdon, spending time with your loved one shows how much you value him and lessens his anxiety and sense of isolation. "'Being with' is the key to providing spiritual care," she says. "This involves spending time with the patient, possibly without speaking. Thoughtful silence, properly used, can be just as effective as words."[11]

Actively listening to the patient is also part of providing spiritual care and support. You don't need to worry about what to say. Concentrate on listening and paying careful attention to his body language and tone of voice. You can follow his lead and be willing to discuss topics of his choice. It is imperative that he be able to talk about his feelings and what he's going through. Be honest and realistic about his situation. If you deny the seriousness of his illness, you may force him to go through it alone emotionally.

Be careful not to pass judgment on your loved one or offer advice. He needs to be heard and understood, not judged. One way to accomplish this is through reflective listening. This can be especially helpful when someone tries to describe his feelings but may need a little help clarifying the cause and effect. The listener summarizes what he has heard and reflects it back to the speaker by saying, "You feel _____ because _____." This type of dialogue can be extremely beneficial.

Your loved one certainly does not need you or anyone else telling him how he should be feeling or what he should be doing to handle his illness better. Accept him wherever he is coming from and try to understand whatever he is sharing with you.

You can also communicate your love and support through the simple act of touch. Find out what feels the best to your loved one. Hold his hand, rub his back, massage his legs, gently tickle his arm, or run your fingers through his hair. Since everyone likes something different, it's usually best to ask what he likes if you don't already know. I remember spending time at my mom's bedside running my fingers through her soft, graying hair. She would close her eyes and look so content. Those were treasured moments for both of us.

Mary Raymer shares some other things that family members should keep in mind as they support a seriously ill patient:

- Listen more; talk less.
- Don't become a parent to your loved one.
- Don't try to minimize your loved one's emotional pain away by saying, "It's okay."

- Try not to take it personally if your loved one is angry or frustrated or if you feel as though you can't do anything right.

Caregivers Need Care, Too

Responding automatically to my mom's low moans, I called out comforting words to her as I sat up in bed. I went into the bathroom for my mini-wake-up routine of splashing cold water on my face, brushing my teeth, and putting on my glasses. Then I walked over to my mom's hospital bed, which we had placed in my parents' bedroom so she could be near us. After checking her morphine pump and emptying and rinsing her stomach bag, I discovered what was wrong. Her gown and sheets needed changing again.

I woke up my sister and together we changed and bathed her for the second time that night. I was so tired that unbearable sensations of nausea were rolling over me, but I kept talking to my mom, encouraging her. *We're almost done, and then I can lay down and rest,* I told myself.

Taking care of an ill loved one is emotionally and physically exhausting, and it's crucial that you take care of yourself. "If you want to be able to help your loved one, you need to take care of yourself by taking breaks and staying healthy," says Raymer. Being healthy means getting enough sleep, exercising, and eating a balanced diet.

One thing I tried to do was to keep working out at a health club. I did not go frequently, but I did manage to pull away a few times for an hour and work up a good sweat. It really did feel good, and it helped me sleep better. I didn't do well in the eating area, however. The first week after I became one of my mom's primary caregivers, I lost more than ten pounds. Food had lost its taste, and with it went my desire to eat. When my mom could no longer eat anything, I started skipping meals even more frequently.

I am thankful for the efforts that my family, including Mom, made to entice me to eat. One person asked, "What good can you be to your mom if you starve yourself to death?" Those were harsh words, but they woke me up to what I was doing. For a long time I ate not because I felt like it, but because I knew I had to.

"Another essential ingredient to taking care of yourself includes being realistic with yourself," says Raymer, who suggests that caregivers learn what to expect in their particular situation. Speaking with a social worker, hospital chaplain, or other experienced person can fill in some of the blanks for caregivers. "Be compassionate with yourself if you get tired or angry," Raymer advises. "Also, try not to feel guilty about how much you do or don't do—you're only human."

Getting lots of support from others will sustain your ability to be a good caregiver. Simply put, you cannot do it all by yourself. For some, accepting help from others is hard for the same reasons it's difficult for a patient to accept help. How many times did I turn down much-needed assistance from people who really did want to pitch in? Way too often. Bite your tongue when you start to say, "No, no, that's okay. We'll be fine. We don't need anything." I could have saved myself a lot of unnecessary strain and stress if I had just learned to say, "Why, that sounds great. Thank you so much for asking!"

You need someone you can talk to about how you are feeling and what you are thinking. The patient need not know every little detail of your worries and fears. If you think that you might have too many emotions for a friend or family member to handle, consider seeing a counselor or social worker who can help you as you care for your loved one. During my mom's illness, I had the listening ears and strong shoulders of my husband, my dad, my sister, and several close girlfriends. I was able to talk and cry with them as I shared my innermost thoughts. They buoyed me when I needed it the most.

Caring for a loved one is a privilege, but it requires stamina, strength, and courage. Don't overlook your resources for support and try to do it on your own. It will work much better with a multitude of helpers and encouragers. By helping you, all of these people are actually helping your loved one.

THE IMPORTANT ROLE OF FRIENDS

Many, if not all, of the suggestions for how family members can support a seriously ill loved one are the same for friends. Just being there and listening are probably the two greatest gifts you can offer your friend.

> *A true friend sticks like glue when life gets rough. May the Lord bless the true friends in this world, and may I learn to be one.*

In *When Your Friend Gets Cancer,* Amy Harwell, a cancer survivor, emphasizes the unique supportive role friends can play. "Though not a substitute for family, friends hold a special niche…friends can listen to fears more readily. Because they are not as dependent on the patient, friends can be less frightened about the consequences of treatment and can usually live better in the ambiguity of the situation," she says.[12]

Friends should try to keep their friendship with the patient as normal as possible. For example, if you both previously liked to attend sporting events, go out to dinner, or see an occasional movie, don't be afraid to continue inviting him. However, you need to be sensitive to any new limitations, physical or otherwise, with which the patient may have to contend. It's important for him to feel involved and part of things in everyday life. I remember my mom going out to lunch, enjoying hikes in the countryside, and taking sightseeing excursions with local and out-of-town friends.

> *After my visit to the doctor on Tuesday, I have felt worse. The reason is that she told me the size of the tumor in the abdomen. I didn't think it was that large. But, the Lord has been encouraging me through friends since then. Marion sent me a wonderful flower arrange-*

ment. Shirley took me to high tea today. Dave and I are planning to go watch the GOES satellite launching. Margaret had me come to lunch with her yesterday. Surely, I have had some very special friends.

Running a household also takes energy and time. If financial circumstances don't permit a patient to hire outside help, friends can step in. Glenn Kirkland cared for his wife, Grace, for thirteen years as she struggled with Alzheimer's disease. He remembers one particular day when a lady from their church called to see if he was home. Shortly after the call, she arrived at the Kirkland's front door with several other people armed with cleaning equipment. Not only did they clean the house from top to bottom, but they also took all the clothes out of Grace's closet. "They brought them back after repairing, washing, and pressing them," says Kirkland, who shed tears over this practical expression of love.

A patient's circle of friends can play important roles in helping him adapt to a new lifestyle. Eugene Clark had a large number of supporters. His coworkers went the extra mile to bring copies of songs and tapes from the office to Eugene's bedside. Friends helped with his care, cleaned the Clarks' house, took care of the children, and even built an addition on their home.

Friends can also fulfill an essential need by helping the rest of the family, including children. Keep your eyes and ears open for opportunities to help—these may or may not be obvious. If your friend is being cared for at home, encourage the caregivers to take time off. Getting away for even a few minutes will provide a good mental break.

Fortunately, when my mom was on hospice care, there were enough family members taking care of her that we were able to relieve one another as needed. Others may not have that option, and friends can offer them relief. They might demur at first, but extend your invitation several times and reassure them that you feel comfortable being alone and know how to handle any potential emergencies.

As a friend, you may want nothing more than to help, but you may not know what to do or what not to do. These dos and don'ts will help.

Do ask him how he is doing.

Do concentrate on him and not on his disease or its side effects.

Do show him compassion and empathy.

Do touch him—hug him; kiss him; hold his hand.

Do suggest something specific that you can do to help him.

Do take the time to really listen and understand what he is saying.

Do talk to him in a normal manner.

Do remember that it's okay to be silent if you're doubtful about what to say.

Do try to be encouraging.

Do offer to pray with or for him.

Don't give any advice or pat answers.

Don't share any horror stories.

Don't say, "Don't worry. Everything will be fine. You'll get better."

Don't ask unanswerable questions like "How long do you have?"

Don't be fatalistic.

Whatever you decide to do to support your friend and his family, keep in mind what an incredible difference it will make. All you have to do is open up your heart to your friend.

FRIENDS WHO DON'T CALL

On the other hand, maybe no one is asking you about your condition, and you are wondering why. Many, many people simply do not know what to say or how to respond to you and therefore may give you the impression that they are avoiding you. Not knowing what to say or the fear of saying the wrong thing usually comes from a lack of experience with sickness and death or a high level of anxiety about dealing with it. Their oversight, whether intentional or not, hurts deeply.

One breast cancer survivor recalls that at the time of her initial diagnosis, and throughout the duration of her chemotherapy treatments, there were several friends who did not call or visit. "At first, I was really upset at their lack of interest and care. How could they just ignore me during a really difficult time? I needed them, and they weren't there for me," she remembers. "Then I realized that they were having a hard time dealing with my illness, not me. But their lack of support still bothers me to this day."

Several years before my mom's illness, the mother of a close friend of mine had a radical mastectomy after being diagnosed with breast cancer. With much regret, I remember that I did absolutely nothing to encourage or help my friend and her family. Why didn't I? It was my first experience with a serious illness, and I did not know what to do or say. I felt uncomfortable and a little afraid. So, I basically ignored the situation and the people in need. I believe that my friend forgave my insensitivity, ignorance, and selfishness years ago, but I fervently pray that I never fall into that trap again.

For the benefit of those friends who truly do want to help you but lack ideas and direction, try to give them specific suggestions so they know exactly what you need. This is easier said than done, especially if you have always prided yourself on an "I-can-do-it-myself" attitude. Friends and family members fishing for clues might say, "If there is anything I can do to help, just let me know." If you can think of an errand or chore that needs to be done, mention it specifically. Instead of coming right out and asking a friend for help, you might try talking about a specific task that is overwhelming you. Most people will pick up on your need at that point and say, "Well, do you think I could help you with that?" Basically, it comes down to allowing your friends and family to step in wherever and whenever necessary. They need you to accept their support.

Even if you make it easy for people to communicate with you about your illness, you may feel that you've done something that has caused a friend to stay away. Remember that it's his problem, not yours. Keep your focus off his disappointing response, and take your hurt to God. Try to glean as much comfort as you can from other friends who are sticking close by. There is always the possibility that the friend who is ignoring you today may become a wonderful support to a future friend in need. Because your insensitive friend will have experienced firsthand what not to do in your situation, he might be better able to show sensitivity and care and love in the future.

"What if we have moved, or there does not seem to be anybody with whom we can be frank and open?" asks Billy Graham. "What then? Remember, the Holy Spirit is praying (Romans 8:26–27, 34). If you're feeling isolated from people and fighting loneliness, remember there is Someone who will never leave or forsake you. God is the only friend who will never disappoint you, ever."[13]

THE BEST HELP OF ALL

It was a cold January morning, but it felt warm in the pre-op room where the nurses were preparing my dad for his radical nephrectomy. "Here is your hospital gown. Take off your glasses and any jewelry. Are these your daughters?" Questions and procedures kept our conversation to a minimum. My sister and I took turns holding his hand and whispering comforting words; however, our own confidence was wavering.

Helplessness. Many of us might use that word to describe how we feel about being able to really help our loved one. What we truly wish is to erase the illness—make it go away. We want our loved one to be out of pain and discomfort. We desire the best medical care for him. We might think that there is nothing we can do for him at times, but we're wrong. Too often we forget how much we can help others by praying for them.

Only minutes before Dad was wheeled away from us, two pastors walked in, each carrying a Bible. One pastor was from my dad's church and the other was from mine. Their prayers visibly moved everyone in the room as they prayed for my dad, my sister and me, and the team of doctors and nurses performing the surgery.

How did these prayers help? My dad recalls: "Although I knew in advance that lots of people would be praying for me at this critical moment, I could actually feel those prayers in an indescribable way. This empowering feeling went way beyond my head knowledge."

Prayer is our communicative link with God, and it can be offered anywhere, at any time, and in any circumstance. It doesn't matter if you live two thousand miles away or next door to your loved one. Far from being a passive activity, prayer changes things.

Prayer dissolves discouragement, worry, and fear. Because God cares about us and loves us, He will help us. A verse I cling to, time and time again, is in Paul's letter to the Philippians. "Be anxious for nothing, but in everything by prayer and supplication with thanksgiving let your requests be made known to God. And the peace of God, which surpasses all comprehension, shall guard your hearts and your minds in Christ Jesus" (Philippians 4:6–7). There are many, many additional promises given to us about how God comforts, strengthens, empowers, listens, saves, forgives, and brings us peace when we ask Him for His help.

Jesus often told His disciples parables to illustrate the truths He modeled for them. He incorporated prayer into every aspect of His life, and when He was preparing His disciples for His death and resurrection, He told them a parable "to show that at all times they ought to pray and not to lose heart" (Luke 18:1).

Prayer changes us. Dr. Stephen Olford, minister emeritus of Calvary Baptist Church in New York City and founder of Olford Ministries International, says that prayer is not overcoming God's reluctance to give, but rather adjusting our wills to the divine will in order that God can righteously hear us and bless us. Therefore, the focus should not be on me and what I want, but on finding out what God wants for me in my life and trusting Him for whatever the outcome. Sometimes these desires can seem to totally contradict each other.

I struggled immensely with this issue during my mom's illness. I prayed wholeheartedly for God to heal her, and I really believed that He could do it. But I did not even want to contemplate the possibility that that might not be His will for her. I was unable to pray for God's will to be accomplished until only weeks before my mom's death. But when I finally was able to truly give up my own wishes and desires in exchange for God's plan, I experienced a different type of peace. I was more at peace with the future.

In light of this, how should we approach praying for a seriously ill loved one? We need not worry that God will reject our prayers if they are not exactly "right." God hears all of our prayers and already knows what is in our hearts. Our prayers do not have to be in a special format or last a certain number of minutes for them to be acceptable to God.

People concerned about how to pray in the midst of suffering should resist getting stuck in the particulars. The authors of *The Complete Idiot's Guide to Prayer* say that there hardly is a wrong way. The point is to do whatever needs to be done to stay connected with God.... So what is the key? "Just do it," say the authors.[14]

You may find it beneficial to consider the following prayer ideas as you pray for your loved one:[15]

- Thank God for who He is and what He does.
- Pray for comfort from excessive pain.

- Pray that God's presence will be known and felt to all those involved.
- Pray for God's peace that surpasses all understanding.
- Pray that God will be glorified despite difficult circumstances.
- Pray for God's grace and strength.
- Pray that God will comfort and take care of the family as well.
- Pray for the family to show sensitivity and genuine love for the patient.

In *Cancer and Faith,* John Carmody talks about the impact his illness had on his faith, and he stresses the importance of prayer. "What the terminally ill most need from their friends is prayer, the token and substance of support at the deepest level..." he writes, "so the people who pray for us out of their depths are our greatest benefactors."[16]

May God bless you as you give your loved one the greatest gift of all—your prayers!

F

PRACTICAL WAYS TO HELP

There are dozens of practical ways to help a loved one who is seriously ill. Many of these suggestions come from patients, their families, and experienced caregivers. Support comes in many different forms and means different things to different people, so don't forget to personalize these ideas and come up with your own customized ways to help. Above everything else, remember how important it is to *show* that you care.

- *Bring complete meals to the family.* Consider using plastic, foil, or other disposable containers. Family members can simply discard them and won't need to worry about washing them or how and when to return them. To spare the family returning dozens of phone calls, one person should coordinate this effort. This person can inform friends of food allergies or preferences and schedule meals. Writing out a weekly schedule of who is bringing what eliminates duplication and helps the family keep things straight when they thank people later.

- *Help with housework.* After my mom's initial diagnosis and surgery, a group of women at her church arranged and paid for a cleaning lady to come once a month during the six months of debilitating chemotherapy treatments that followed.

- *Help with yardwork.* If you see that the lawn needs mowing, mow it. You can rake leaves, weed, water the grass—whatever needs to be done.

- *Run errands and shop.* Mail packages or letters, pick up prescriptions at the drugstore, and buy needed grocery items. One lady always called us before heading out the door to do her grocery shopping. We almost always needed something, and she bought it for us. When she brought it over, she made a note of how much it cost, and we paid her back later.

- *Offer to take care of children of the patient or of the patient's family.* You could take them to the zoo or McDonald's, or just watch them for a few short hours. Driving kids to school, lessons, or other activities would undoubtedly be of great help. Be sensitive to parents who feel pulled in two directions. Because of guilt or not wanting to put you out, they may have a difficult time letting go of their kids.

- *Write a letter or send a special card of encouragement.* When my mom couldn't read the cards herself, we read them to her and showed her the front of each one. Every day she looked forward to our afternoon reading session. Afterwards, we left the cards by her bedside for her to go through later. Those cards reinforced her belief that people really cared for her. We all enjoyed reading letters that evoked memories of the past and the selected Bible verses that friends sent to comfort us. One son wrote to all of his father's longtime friends and asked them to write him letters recalling old, fun times and encouraging him. His ailing father appreciated this tremendously.

- *Bring a magazine or book for the patient to read.*
- *Bring fresh cut flowers, potted plants, or a silk flower arrangement.* Before you bring live plants or flowers, find out if the patient has any restrictions or preferences. My mom couldn't have live plants around after her chemotherapy treatment. Another woman was adamant that no one send her flowers because she felt that flowers made the room look like a funeral parlor.
- *Bring nature to your loved one.* One of my mom's friends who regularly sent her cards would often enclose a dried, pressed flower from her garden. What a special memento!
- *Send a care package.* It could include a special memento, a tape or CD, an encouraging sermon on tape, a book, a framed picture of the two of you, or other small gift.
- *Help your loved one look nice.* You could wash, brush, or curl a woman's hair, or give her a manicure or pedicure. Find out what would make her feel really good about herself and her appearance. You could help a man by holding a mirror so he can shave in bed, or give him a bottle of his favorite cologne.
- *Give your loved one a gift certificate for a massage.*
- *Call and visit frequently.* Keep phone calls and visits brief unless you are asked to stay or you sense you are needed. Respect privacy.
- *Offer to help file medical bills and insurance claims.* This is such an important task, but it's often neglected or done poorly when there is so much else going on. If you are an organized, detail-oriented person, you could spare the family an onerous task and save the patient and the family money.
- *Fill up his car with gas and have it washed and waxed.*

- *Offer to go with the patient to a doctor's appointment or therapy.* Having someone to wait with in the lobby or waiting room can be a big relief. You may want to bring a book to read so that the patient doesn't feel obligated to talk with you the whole time.
- *Offer to write for him.* You could write out thank-you notes or anything else he might want you to do.
- *Send a balloon bouquet.* Children are not the only ones who love them! You could bring just one special balloon to your loved one when you visit. It's a great icebreaker.
- *Create a special basket of lotions and personal care products.* Skin can get very dry in a hospital environment. Be sure to check beforehand if the person is allergic or sensitive to any perfumes, dyes, or other ingredients.
- *Bring a coffee mug filled with individual packets of gourmet coffee, or a teacup with herb teas.* You could add cinnamon sticks, biscotti, or hot chocolate packets.
- *Help your loved one stay in touch with church, local, and national news.* Clip newspaper articles of interest, save cartoons, or collect church bulletins.
- *Bring a stuffed animal.* Most people appreciate one—even men! It can be a soft companion in a hospital bed.

PART III

JOURNEY'S END

For four and a half years we have been on a journey together. I was the wounded wanderer; you were they who bound my wounds and encouraged me to continue the trip. The journey, for me, is now over and the victory is won! I could not have done it alone.

Jesus was my constant companion and all of you never left my side.... I learned a great deal through each of you and often I saw Jesus in your ministry to me and my family. Certainly this is what life is all about—the learning to love one another as Christ has loved us. Yes, there are earthly pleasures along the way—a foretaste of the blessings to come—but they should never become the focus. We must learn to sacrifice for one another and love each other in preparation for the perfection required of us in heaven....

I look forward to rejoicing with you in eternity.

"Do not fear, for I have redeemed you;
I have called you by name; you are Mine!
When you pass through the waters, I will be with you;
And through the rivers, they will not overflow you.
When you walk through the fire, you will not be scorched,
Nor will the flame burn you.
For I am the LORD your God."

ISAIAH 43:1–3

———◆◆◆———

F
Since I am coming to that holy room
where, with the choir of saints forevermore,
I shall be made thy music;
as I come I tune the instrument here at the door,
and what I must do then, think now before.

JOHN DONNE

EIGHT

Each Moment of Each Day

E ven though the sun beat down relentlessly on the dry ground, I felt icy cold. The events of the previous day raced through my mind as I stood in my backyard watering the parched flowers. Millions of droplets brushed each leaf and petal. The ground was so hard that most of the water couldn't soak in right away, just as my mind couldn't soak in what was happening to my mom. I kept asking myself, *So, this is it then? How could the end come so soon? What is going to happen next? How can I live without her?*

Whenever I reflect on that week in August 1994, I still feel cold and alone. After four and a half years of battling ovarian cancer, my mom was told that an enlarged tumor was blocking her intestinal tract. Medically speaking, there was nothing more to do but offer her comfort and take measures to control the pain.

I hadn't known all the medical facts of the progression of her disease. She had chosen to keep them from me while she still could because she didn't want me to worry. However, if I had really thought about why she stopped treatments—they were no longer working—I would have realized how close the end was. I think that I was in denial until her final hospitalization in August.

Excerpts from my mom's journal between late June and early August chronicle her growing realization that her journey was finally coming to an end.

The CA-125 was up to over 190 in spite of the treatments that are wiping out my blood. So the treatments are over. There will not be much time left. It is totally in the Lord's hands (as if it has not been for four years).

The key is to remain firmly in the Scriptures. The Lord will give me the strength I need for each new day. Helen shared with me about how her husband died of cancer—how the Lord strengthened him until the end. It was very encouraging.

Yesterday I had my last C/T scan. What a relief that all the procedures, operations and treatments are over. Now I am directly in the hands of the Lord—no cushions. I am satisfied for the Lord's way is perfect. I'll not leave until the time is absolutely right. That is why I must never pre-anticipate my departure.

In fact, I feel some kind of excitement for the journey. It will be the journey of my life—the one for which I have prepared for 52 years! You might say, it will be an experience of a lifetime!

This afternoon I was sitting in the car at the mall waiting for Dave to run an errand. It was raining and the sound on the roof reminded me of all those times we went camping, and it rained on the tent. Then I thought how I am possibly only weeks away from death now. How can things feel so normal and yet be drawing to an end? What new sounds will there be in the next life? Will I be aware of the passage? Can I watch the translation from time to eternity take place? What will I remember of this life?

The events of recent days have left me breathless—the anticipated trip to the reunion of the family, the intestinal blockage, and trip to the emergency room of St. Vincent Hospital [in Green Bay, Wisconsin], and finally the marathon drive back to Gaithersburg, arriving at 1 a.m. on Thursday morning. All of this led to my present hospitalization.

Once again I thought I would die, and once again I will be snatched from the jaws of death. How difficult this is for the family. Poor Patricia thinks I am dying for sure.

I can't help but think about our aborted trip. The Lord said, "Look at Nancy, she is looking forward to some fun. I think it's time for another trial." Lord, forgive me for seeing this in such a negative light. Help me to have the eyes to accept that Your way is actually the better one. Faith tells me that I must see things differently. Certainly to blame You for destroying my fun is sin.

Lord, I will accept this new trouble and trust You to use it to purify me even more. I will not become embittered. I do not understand it, but I know that You can turn something bad into something good.

TIME IS SHORT NOW

When my mom was hospitalized for the final time, my dad, sister, and I worked together like a real team. We didn't even need to discuss certain things with one another at length because we all knew what needed to be done. Compared to that first hospital stay, we knew the ropes.

On the other hand, nothing can ever totally prepare someone for a physician's statement: "Sorry, there's nothing more we can do—your disease is terminal." Those words have tremendous power and signal a major shift in your medical team's plan of care and the future of your family and yourself.

Once a terminal prognosis is given, patients may experience emotions and reactions very similar to those they had when they were first diagnosed. This time, the feelings, behaviors, and thoughts could be even more intense for the patient and the family, as each person again moves through a variety of emotional, physical, psychological, and spiritual stages.

Mary Raymer says that every patient reacts differently when the fight to be cured becomes the fight to maintain the highest quality of life possible. Some individuals are very relieved at the thought of not having more treatments and procedures. Many patients *do* feel better physically than they have for a long time, she adds, simply because they are not going through aggressive treatments.

With the cessation of medical treatment, care shifts from curative to palliative. What is palliative care? The World Health Organization says that it is the active, total care of patients whose disease is not responsive to curative treatment. Its goal is to achieve the best possible quality of life for patients and their families through control of pain and other symptoms and the treatment of psychological, social, and spiritual problems. Palliative care:

- affirms life and regards dying as a normal process;
- neither hastens nor postpones death;
- provides relief from pain and other distressing symptoms;
- integrates the psychological and the spiritual aspects of care;
- offers a support system to help patients live as actively as possible until death;
- offers a support system to help the family cope during the patient's illness and in their own bereavement.[1]

With the shift to palliative care, grief can hit some patients hard because they are no longer fighting for a cure. Others quickly accept the reality of the terminal illness and focus on what gives their life meaning in the time remaining.

Sadly, some patients never know that the nature of their care has changed from curative to palliative because the medical establishment or their family either doesn't want to tell them or doesn't want to abandon what have become futile treatments. "Many act as if a patient will 'give up' the minute we shift to palliative, and that is the root of why people do not get referred to good palliative care," says Raymer. "Some people do give up; but from my experience, most don't."

What happens when patients don't know that their prognosis is terminal? According to Dr. Daniel Haffey, not acknowledging impending death can prevent or inhibit them from dying well. He also believes that they should not be distracted with unfounded hopes for miracle cures. Instead, "they should be enabled to make the most of the time that's left and spend meaningful times with their family."

When it becomes clear that time is short, patients and their families need to accept the inevitable. Katharine G. Baker says that the acceptance of the limitations of medical intervention and of human mortality should not diminish the patient's potential for continuing emotional growth up until the very moment of death.[2]

Marjory Purvis urges families and friends to be open and willing to talking about a loved one's death. "I remember that if I mentioned my daughter's name, people would change the subject. They didn't want to talk about it because they thought it would upset me," she says. What Marjory really wanted was to discuss it, but even members of her own family did not want to (and in many ways could not) talk about it. "I think everyone was just so busy trying to handle his own grief," she adds.

What are some helpful things you can do to cope with this new phase of your health situation as you make the transition from curative to palliative care?

As a patient, you can:

- Be willing to discuss realistically the status and results of your treatments with your physician. Remember that it's okay to stop treatments—you are not a failure.
- Realize that your acceptance of your mortality will ease the way for family members to accept it, too.
- Complete your advance directives and living will. Discuss your wishes with your medical-care team as well as with your family.
- Allow yourself to grieve.
- Talk to a close friend, family member, social worker, psychologist, chaplain, or pastor about your feelings, thoughts, and desires.
- Discuss changes in your relationships with your spouse, children, and other family members. Keep in mind that social roles and relationships will change throughout your illness.
- Ensure that financial planning is completed. Make sure that your spouse and, if applicable, adult children have no questions about any aspect of your estate.
- Discuss any other specifics about your wishes and have them written down.
- Set small goals and make them realistic. (Don't forget to prioritize.)
- Enjoy the little things in life—watching a sunrise or sunset; listening to friends and family members tell jokes; feeling the squeeze of a hand or the softness of a kiss.
- Consider your options for palliative care, including hospice programs.

As a family member or friend, you can:

- Allow your loved one time to digest the news.
- Be patient and allow your loved one to dictate the pace of adjustment.
- Be willing to talk about death and dying with your loved one.
- Be sensitive to your loved one's feelings in this area and respect

his wishes, accepting that they may be different from your own.

- Do not minimize your loved one's pain as he grieves.
- Be there.
- Touch your loved one physically when you communicate, and give lots of hugs. (Ask permission first to ensure that it does not cause physical discomfort or pain.)
- Be silent.
- Let your loved one stay as involved as possible in household affairs. This will help sustain self-esteem and a sense of control.
- Hold a family conference as a way of planning how to divide responsibilities.
- Be careful about talking about your loved one in hushed tones in another room. Would you like to be whispered about?
- If you sense that treatments are not effecting a cure but no palliative care options are being discussed, talk to the doctor and ask questions. (This is only for spouses or immediate family members.)
- Seek outside support, even if your loved one has not accepted that death is inevitable.

GRIEVING THE LOSS OF HOPES AND DREAMS

One evening, during that last week of August 1994, I stopped at a drugstore to pick up several prescriptions for my mom. My dad, sister, and I took turns running errands and being with her. She was growing weaker. While waiting for the pharmacist to fill the prescriptions, I paced the aisles looking for nothing in particular. After glancing at one of the pill bottles, I looked at the date and, shocked, quickly added a home pregnancy test to my purchases.

It is hard to think about, but Josh will never remember me. Any further grandchildren of either Lori or Becky will never have known me at all. How sad.

I cried tears of sorrow when I saw the results. I knew that my mom was only days away from death. As I knelt beside the rented hospital bed in my parents' bedroom to tell her about this new grandchild growing in my womb, I was taken aback by her response. "That's perfect," she said. "Absolutely perfect."

If I am really honest, my desires remain selfish. I want to be close to my daughters and their families and help them with their babies and be a grandmother. I must be willing to die to this desire. Only then do I have the freedom to be what the Lord wants me to be!

How could it be perfect? I wondered. My own response had been one of sadness mixed with anger. Sadness because she would never even get to meet my unborn baby, let alone watch him grow into adulthood. Anger because she was leaving me when I wanted and needed her most. Her lack of bitterness amazed me. She seemed content just with knowing the news.

I certainly did not feel content with the situation. I wanted my children to have her as their grandmother for a long time. I needed to grieve *my* loss of a future hope and dream. *Suddenly, there were no more tomorrows.* All I had with her was today.

One way I dealt with this was to remind myself how wonderful it was that my older son did get to meet and spend eighteen months with her. Also, I felt extremely thankful that I was able to share the news of my pregnancy. The timing was incredible. I told her on Friday, and she went into a coma on Sunday.

Another way I faced the future without my dream was to remember the rich legacy my mom was leaving behind. Our memories were full of marvelous moments and experiences together over the years. She had been a wonderful mother, and I became even more inspired to continue her legacy. I made a promise to God and myself: *I will strive to be the best godly mother I can be, just like Mom was.* I also vowed to keep the memory of her alive in my children. Today, my children know that they have one grandmother who lives in Tennessee and one who lives in heaven.

My mom spent precious time writing a letter to Joshua before she died. She left it on a computer disk for us to read after her death. Even though it is addressed to him, it is also for all her other unborn grandchildren. It allowed her to communicate with them in the future that she would not live to see, and it was very important to her to share these important thoughts with them.

I treasure her letter, and I wish that my dad, sister, and I had thought about archiving more of her thoughts for us or for grandchildren to come. We could have helped her write things down or recorded them on audio or videotapes.

Terminally ill patients and their families grieve different lost dreams and dashed hopes. What future hopes or dreams are you grieving right now?

- Being a mother/father/grandmother/grandfather
- Missing a child/grandchild's special days (baptism, birthday, graduation, wedding)
- Retiring with your husband or wife
- Pursuing a hobby or vocation
- Traveling to _____
- Buying a _____
- Reaching the pinnacle of your career
- Fulfilling a lifelong dream
- Never having _____
- Never doing _____

People grieve these losses in different ways. Raymer says that one of the best ways to grieve the loss of a future hope or dream is to acknowledge that it is no longer possible and to talk about what is. "Everybody wants to be remembered," she says. "We all want to know that we've touched someone, even if we're alone. If there is no hope for a future, ask yourself, 'What is the hope for *today?*'"

What can you do about dreams that are just not possible, like becoming a grandparent or being present at your daughter's wedding or graduation? Accepting the inevitable does not mean that you resign yourself to zero involvement. You could share some of your thoughts with your family about any of these anticipated big events. I am sure your words will be forever etched in their memories and that they will cherish them when the event occurs.

You may not live to see grandchildren, but you could do something for them right now, like reading them a story. Consider recording a special story on audio or videocassette and giving it to your son or daughter to keep for later. Or you might want to write a letter or even make a videotape of yourself giving words of wisdom or encouragement about a future event. You could also give a family heirloom *now* in honor of a future wedding, a child's birth, or a graduation ceremony. In this way, you can feel that you're a part of the future.

What about the things that are possible? Ask yourself what you would most like to do. Is there anything you would like to make sure you've accomplished should your death come sooner than you think? You can gain a great deal of satisfaction from completing even one task or project that's important to you.

My mom loved knitting things for us. That last summer she asked my sister and me if we would like to have either an afghan or a sweater. Rebecca selected a delicate afghan pattern, and I chose a sweater. With lots and lots of love and determination, Mom knit both out of the same off-white yarn. She finished them barely two weeks before she died. I know that she felt good about being able to make us something really special. And now whenever I wear my hand-knit sweater, its warmth makes me feel her loving arms wrapped tightly around me.

Family members and friends need to be sensitive to a loved

one's grieving of future hopes and dreams. You can encourage him to talk about what's important to him and what it is he is grieving. You could play an important role in helping him live some of his dreams. Encourage him to do as much as he possibly can whenever he is able. Figure out if you could help him realize some of his dreams, even if it's on a small scale.

This is an incredible opportunity for you to be creative. I remember that one of my mom's friends, who knew how much she had wanted to see a specific performer in concert, spent the time videotaping the live performance on TV. She brought it over for my mom to watch at home. How thoughtful!

Be careful to follow the patient's lead in this area of future hopes and dreams. If you sense a large amount of anxiety, tread carefully. You need to be sensitive to how your loved one is feeling about the future. He probably feels left out. Wouldn't you? Respect your loved one's wishes for privacy, and be available for encouragement without being pushy.

KEEPING AN ETERNAL PERSPECTIVE

In Hannah Hurnard's classic allegory *Hinds' Feet on High Places,* Much-Afraid encounters dangers and fears in her spiritual journey to the High Places. Sorrow and Suffering are her companions throughout the long, painful ascent. Along the way she collects stones to remind herself of each hardship and the choice she made to accept and endure the loving Shepherd's way of escape for her.

Imagine her surprise at the transformation of the dull rocks at journey's end:

> Then she gasped again with bewilderment and delight, for instead of the common, ugly stones she had gathered from the altars along the way, there fell into her hands a heap of glorious, sparkling jewels, very precious and very beautiful.[3]

Each of these jewels was then set in a crown and placed upon her head.

What an incredible way of looking at earthly afflictions and sufferings! You are not just enduring a momentary affliction; you are building a heavenly inheritance.

How is it possible to view pain and suffering in the context of eternity? In 1918 Helen Lemmel wrote a hymn that tells how: "Turn your eyes upon Jesus, look full in His wonderful face, and the things of earth will grow strangely dim in the light of His glory and grace."[4] If your eyes are on Jesus, it will be easier to trust in His promises for your eternal hope. Looking at life through the lens of eternity can change our perspective on earthly struggles.

> *Finally, we will look at what our focus should be—the eternal life. If life here on earth is 100 years or less, how does that compare to eternity? Most of us cannot comprehend the infinite but we can at least see that there is no comparison between infinity and less than 100. Certainly, then we should try to be prepared for the life that will be with us the longest. What can we expect? How can we prepare for it?*

Eternity in the presence of God begins for you on the day you choose to open yourself to Jesus Christ. Then, says Rev. Timothy D. Crater, "His Spirit indwells you; His love surrounds you. Heaven will be tomorrow's physical realization of today's spiritual reality."[5]

Concentrating on eternity can help you identify what really matters in life. In Matthew 6:33, Jesus says that our top priority in life should be to seek first His kingdom and His righteousness. Too often, when people are healthy and successful, they lose their focus. They don't seem to need God, and they don't consult, or even remember, Him unless a problem arises. They make their plans well into the future without thinking about living for today and really enjoying each moment.

Throughout His earthly ministry, Jesus emphasized the importance of doing what God wants you to do (Matthew 6:10; 16:24–28). Dying to self is seldom easy because it requires you to set aside your own wishes and replace them with God's desires for you. At times, Jesus Himself struggled with doing His Father's will instead of His own (Luke 22:42).

Rev. Mark Tindle believes that being satisfied with today comes from continually viewing life from an eternal perspective. He says, "We should ask God daily, 'What do You have for me to do today?' But we rarely do that because we're too busy investing our time in next month or next year." We all have the luxury of avoiding this question when we are healthy, Tindle adds, but terminal illness puts it in the limelight because tomorrow may never come.

You have a choice today about how you will spend your hours and minutes. One of the best ways to stay in tune with what God wants you to do is to continually deepen your relationship with Him. Spend time in prayer. Read your Bible. If these activities are impossible, simply rest in God and let His spirit comfort, strengthen, and bring peace to you. Never lose sight of your goal—your citizenship in heaven—and keep reaching forward to what lies ahead (Philippians 3:13–14). In heaven your body will be transformed into conformity with the body of His glory (Philippians 3:20–21).

I'm finally beginning to see that this life is so short—it's not worth wasting on selfish desires. The next life is the one to delight in. So spend this life preparing for the next.

Several months ago I thought I was soon to die. At that point, suddenly I knew what it meant to die to self. I also had a totally different feeling for this life.

No longer did things of this life matter. As soon as my cancer was recognized as shrinking, and I realized I was not going to die just yet, I lost the vision I had received for the next world and its true relationship to this one.

Suddenly, I once more had to think in terms of taking care of worldly things and they began to matter again. I think I liked the freedom of the death notice. I don't want to care for the worldly things.

Without the hope of an eternal future with God, how is a person with a serious or terminal illness to feel hopeful? A worldly hope is based on good health and good circumstances or, in the face of adversity, standing strong against it. But this earthly existence is not all there is to life. After trying every earthly avenue for lasting pleasure and contentment, King Solomon concluded that everything in life is meaningless except fearing God and obeying His commandments (Ecclesiastes 12:13).

After logging countless hours in clinics and doctors' offices over a span of several years, my mom wrote this poem on what she had observed:

Faces in the Clinic

They come in hope,
These faces in the clinic.
The fresh faces encouraged,
but those from many months
    look tired.
They've seen so much
    of waiting,
    of disappointment,
    of recurrence.
Still they cling to hope

as the one last thread
   tying them to this existence.
For they have seen the result
   of hope lost:
Those faces gone—forever.

Because my citizenship is in heaven, not on earth (Philippians 3:19), being hopeful about what happens after death is not escapism. I was created to bring glory to God, and in heaven I will do that for eternity. I am being realistic about my future when I concentrate on what I should be doing today in light of my eternal hope in Jesus (1 Corinthians 3:10–15).

I have come to see things in a new light. I am, in fact, blessed because I can see things in the light of eternity. For too long I had intellectualized the imminence of death and delegated it to some place far in the future. This can never be true in this life.

Every one of us, me included, is untouchable by death until the Lord's time for us. I know no more nor less of the time of my death than I did before I was faced with this deadly disease. The difference, then, is only now it brings the fact of life's lack of guarantee to the forefront, and I can live as I am supposed to live—one day at a time—trusting God for whatever lies ahead.

F

HOW CAN I BE SATISFIED WITH TODAY?

Knowing that your eternal perspective is based on hope, how can you really learn to be satisfied with only today? You can find satisfaction in today because God is walking with you, regardless of the circumstances. The following promises from the Bible can help you focus on attaining true contentment and peace as your physical health wanes:

- You can cast your burden on God, and He has promised to sustain you (Psalm 55:22).
- You do not have to be afraid because God is with you (Isaiah 41:10).
- You can enjoy God's lovingkindnesses and compassions every morning (Lamentations 3:22–23).
- You can come to God for rest (Matthew 11:28).
- You can receive what God desires for you by sacrificing your own desires (Luke 22:42).
- You can experience God's love anytime, anywhere—nothing can take that away from you (Romans 8:38–39).
- You will not be broken, even though you may be feeling crushed inside (2 Corinthians 4:8–10).
- You can be thankful that your citizenship is in heaven (Philippians 3:19).
- You can pray to God and have your anxiety transformed into the peace of God (Philippians 4:6–7).
- You can be content with whatever you have and with whichever situation faces you (Philippians 4:11–12).
- You can do all things through Him who strengthens you (Philippians 4:13).
- You can draw near to God, and He has promised to draw near to you (James 4:8).
- You can endure the sufferings of this world in light of the glory that is to come (1 Peter 1:3–7).

I will give thanks to Thee,
for I am fearfully and wonderfully made....
Thine eyes have seen my unformed substance;
and in Thy book they were all written,
the days that were ordained for me,
when as yet there was not one of them.

Psalm 139:14, 16

———◆———

F
Most of us have a subliminal desire to leave this world
with some degree of dignity...quick, quiet, easy.
But life doesn't follow the pattern
we have so clumsily designed....
Death has many faces and voices.

Billy Graham

NINE

Grace and Acceptance

T he noise of the ventilator pump rose above his pleading voice. "It's me, Steven. I'm right here," my husband said to Besta, his ninety-year-old Norwegian grandmother. "If you can hear me, squeeze my hand.... I love you. I'll always love you."

Besta spent two and a half weeks in an intensive care unit before she died. The agony of watching her cling to life by means of machines and plastic tubing was almost unbearable. Until the moment of her death, her family had to make decisions about procedures that could sustain or possibly prolong her life.

Although advances in medical technology have enabled people to live longer than ever before, they have also raised more questions about end-of-life decisions. In *A Different Death*, Edward J. Larson and Darrel W. Amundsen note that although people can now survive serious accidents and degenerative diseases for a significant period of time, they often do so in a coma or other incapacitated state. "These situations," they say, "can raise profound questions about when to end treatment—questions that arose less often in an earlier era.... Today over 85 percent of all Americans die in a hospital, and in many of these cases somebody must make a decision to stop further medical treatment."[1]

THE PHYSICIAN-ASSISTED SUICIDE DEBATE

In recent years, the need to make these decisions has led to heated debates about physician-assisted suicide, which became legal in Oregon in 1997. Several other states are now considering making it legal, and the outcome will directly affect the futures of terminally ill patients and their families.[2]

What is the difference between euthanasia and physician-assisted suicide? Dr. David L. Stevens, executive director of the Christian Medical and Dental Associations, makes the following distinctions:

> **Passive euthanasia** is the withholding or withdrawing of support without the patient's consent, with the intent of causing death.
>
> **Active euthanasia** is the voluntary (with consent), nonvoluntary (consent not possible), or involuntary (consent possible, but not sought) intentional termination of the patient's life.
>
> **Physician-assisted suicide** is the patient's voluntary taking of his own life with the assistance of a doctor who provides the means.

Stevens emphasizes that there are certain situations in which potentially life-prolonging treatments should be withheld or withdrawn because they are futile. "When medical intervention is simply prolonging the death process, it needs to be reevaluated," he says. "With our advanced technology, there is always one more thing we can do even in the face of little or no hope. Doctors and families need to realize that when everything reasonable has been done, it is time to let the patient die."

The authors of *Life and Death Decisions* clarify this when they state that it is not passive euthanasia to allow a patient to die naturally by withholding or withdrawing treatment. "We would say that withdrawing or withholding treatment or artificial means of life support in someone who is dying is not euthanasia at all—not even passive euthanasia—but acceptable, humane, and an often necessary part of everyday medical practice."[3]

Physician-assisted suicide, however, is not about giving the patient the right to die. "It's about giving doctors the right to kill," Stevens says. That is an enormous difference, because in this case "the doctor becomes judge, jury, and assistant executioner."

As I watch the ceremonies of Nixon's death, I can't help but think of my own approaching death. I have done nothing noteworthy in the broader scene. But has my life been meaningful to anyone other than myself? We come to this earth to become—whatever is the Lord's design. Some of us achieve this lofty goal. Others of us never even know it is a goal. Whether we know it or not, we all prepare for this last trip. I am still counted among the living although my heart and desires already reside among the dead. I have seen enough of the pain and misery and look toward the day the Lord pronounces it "enough." I no longer even remember what it was like to live a "normal" life.

I saw no indication that my mom ever thought about suicide during the course of her illness. Of course, she had her "down" days. Moments of sadness, grief, self-pity, and frustration came and went throughout the years she battled cancer. Bouts of depression appeared to grip her more tightly at some times than at others, but they were never predictable as to length or intensity. My entire family experienced similar emotional roller-coaster rides.

I don't want to die so that I can be with Him, but rather so that I can escape life. Why else would I feel relief at the time I found out I was going to die? Why else would I immediately set out planning my funeral? I may still be going to die, but I must change my reason for wanting to die. My attitude must be for the desire for Him, not my fear of life.

It is wrong, however, to assume that a person with a strong faith would never want to commit suicide. "Terminally ill patients have every reason to be depressed," says Stevens. "They are dying. And Christians are not immune. The 'will to live' can vary even within the same day in terminally ill patients."

Mary Raymer believes that, in fact, it is a rare terminally ill patient who does not think about suicide. "If a patient has proper love and support, he can work through this and find a reason to live until he dies," she says. Stevens observes that terminally ill patients who experience suicidal desires are really questioning whether life is still worthwhile. This is where family members and the patient's medical team can step up and offer support.

I was thinking today that I certainly have been pruned. When I think that there were times when I would have ended my life had there been a clean way to do it that would look like an accident, I would not have been able to provide the support for Dave that he needs right now.

In a letter she wrote to the editor of the *Washington Post,* my mom made clear her views on physician-assisted suicide.

As a terminal cancer patient, I have several reasons for thinking that doctor-assisted suicide should never be legalized.

The doctor-patient relationship is special, and there is a subtle change in the patient's attitude when he feels that the doctor no longer thinks that his life is worth continuing.

Even if the patient brings up the subject, the fact that the doctor would agree to assist in the suicide sends a message to the patient that the doctor agrees that this life is not worth continuing. It is enough to encourage the patient to quit.

If a person is contemplating suicide alone, often a certain restraint keeps him from carrying it out. However, if that person is being assisted in bringing about the suicide, there is a subtle strengthening of the resolve by the very presence of the other person who is doing the assisting. Difficult tasks are easier to perform when one has a partner in the act.

I have a high view of life on earth. We are here for a purpose. If this were not so, why shouldn't every one of us commit suicide whenever life gets tough? It is not only terminally ill people who experience despair and helplessness. Because there is a reason each of us is here, we have certain opportunities to fulfill this purpose. It is through suffering that we question who we are, who God is, and whether we should have a relationship with Him. If a person chooses to leave this earth without the suffering that God thinks is best for him, it might turn out that he faces an eternity of suffering rather than just the short temporal suffering he would have had here on this earth.

People seem to have lost sight of the fact that a successful life is not making a lot of money or having a good time. The person who dies with the most toys does not win. Rather it is the person who has found God's love and has learned to love others who gets the prize. Often this can only be learned through suffering. Let's not make it easier for him to fail.

Nancy S. Seiler

I hated watching my mom die. Even though her fight against metastasized cancer lasted for years, the active dying process lasted only a few weeks. With each passing day, her physical body deteriorated as the cancer grew stronger.

Nevertheless, throughout those final days, I never once had a desire to hasten her death. Even though the experience was horrible, I felt an inner peace from God Almighty. I rested, sometimes in turmoil, in His sovereignty. I also spent many treasured moments with her that last month—moments full of hugs, kisses, laughter, family memories, comforting words, backrubs, advice, and dreams. I never would have wanted her in the hands of a physician anxious to end her suffering by causing her death. She was already cradled in God's loving arms.

HANDLING DEPRESSION AND PAIN

Untreated depression can make any seriously ill person want to die. A 1995 Canadian study on terminally ill patients found that, compared to those with no desire to die prematurely, patients expressing a wish to die were depressed. "The results," say the investigators, "indicate that many terminally ill patients who express death wishes might benefit from treatment for psychological distress."[4]

Mary Raymer says that if the terminally ill are not treated aggressively enough for depression and that if patients are depressed or have some other existing pathology that is not being treated, they will probably want to die.

Stevens wholeheartedly agrees. Although it may be difficult for caregivers to pinpoint depression in their loved one because of physiological changes brought about by a disease, "physicians need to be able to recognize depression and treat it aggressively to the very end." He suggests that family members and medical professionals pay close attention to a loved one's sleeping and eating habits. Decreased appetite, changes in bowel habits, not sleeping well, suicidal comments, and lack of joy from things that normally cause joy (such as visits from grandchildren) could be signs of depression. Depression is treatable in the terminally ill, sometimes with and sometimes without medication.

My life is slowly being filled with pain and discomfort. I can see that, depending on how long this must be endured, could bring on a desire to end it all.

Besides depression, pain can lead seriously ill patients to think about committing suicide. According to the 1999 report of the State of Oregon Health Division, the three most important reasons that patients request physician-assisted suicide are loss of autonomy or decreasing quality of life, becoming a burden to friends and family, and worsening pain. "Pain or the fear of pain is a driving factor in requests for assisted suicide. Studies show that the number of requests for assisted suicide drop dramatically when more effective approaches to pain and suffering are employed."[5]

Pain is *not* something patients should learn to live with, says social worker Joanne Morton. "It can be managed by health-care professionals." Here she corrects two common misconceptions about the management of pain.

• **Too much medication will cause addiction.**
When one is addicted, there is a psychological or emotional dependence on feeling "high." Seriously ill people do not take drugs to get high, but to relieve their pain. When the proper dosage of medication is taken around the clock, addiction does not occur. If they take it properly, patients can take pain medication indefinitely and not become addicted.

• **Too much medication will cause patients to need higher and higher dosages, until eventually no dosage will work.**
Caregivers will work to find the right treatment or combination of

medications to keep patients free and alert so they can have quality of life.

In order to help keep their pain under control, Morton suggests that patients describe it to their doctor or nurse in detail. "Words like *sharp, burning, dull,* and *aching* or *mild, moderate,* and *severe* will help," she says. "Identifying a scale of one to five or one to ten and attaching a number to your pain can also be helpful." Patients or a caregiver can keep a diary of pain—when it begins, when it peaks, when the patient takes medications, and how much helps.[6]

A health-care team has many different options for controlling and managing physiological pain. "There is always something more that can be done. Don't let your family member suffer," says Stevens. "Different kinds of pain respond better to different medicines. If a physician cannot control pain adequately, insist on a consultation with a pain specialist."

The authors of *Hospice and Palliative Care* say that patient choice also plays a role. "Some patients choose to have pain at a very low level of discomfort in order to maintain function, while others may choose to have pain completely relieved and may accept sedation as a side effect of complete relief. The patient rightfully remains in control of this decision regarding care as long as possible and practical."[7]

Physiological pain is not the only kind of pain a patient deals with at the end of life. "The psychological aspect needs to be recognized," says Dr. Gilbert Gonzales, whose expertise lies in the management of pain. "We need to be vigorous about treating symptoms, and this includes the psychological." He asks every patient about the psychological aspect because he believes that "if you have pain, you will have major psychological effects of that pain."

Pain management, symptom relief, and depression can be effectively addressed in the terminally ill. Keep communicating with your physician, family, friends, and clergy as you cope with your illness, including any suicidal thoughts. Let them know how you are feeling physically as well as emotionally.

> *Lord, what is this? Are You asking me to live as a dead person without the pleasure of food? Am I to slowly starve to death? If, indeed, this is what is being asked of me, I must learn to live in obedience. I can think of nothing more difficult than this for me.*

Supporters of physician-assisted suicide often talk about the need to be compassionate and the patient's right to die. But Stevens asks how mercy killing can be compassionate when it relieves the doctor and the family of their burden of compassion. He says:

> The most important thing a doctor can say to a patient and his family is "I'm going to be here with you through this and help control your symptoms and eliminate your suffering." Those of us in health care should never say, "Well, we've done all we can," when a patient is dying. The patient needs us more than ever. This is when real intensive care takes place. During one of the most difficult times of the patient's life, we should not only control their symptoms, but we should also give them emotional, social, and spiritual support.

Gonzales says that families of seriously ill patients often make decisions about assisted suicide from their armchairs instead of from personal experience. He has heard younger family members say, "I will kill myself if I ever get in that kind of condition." Yet when some of these same family members are later struck with a serious illness, they decide to struggle to keep living.

If you or your loved one are faced with difficult decisions about end-of-life care, keep the following Bible verses in mind as you discuss possibilities with your medical-care team.[8]

- You are of inestimable value, made in the very image of God (Genesis 1:27; 1 John 4:9–10).
- Murder breaks God's commandment (Exodus 20:13; Leviticus 24:17); suicide is self-murder.
- God is sovereign over life, death, and judgment. Suicide takes into your hands what belongs in God's hands (Deuteronomy 32:39; Job 12:10; Psalm 139:16; Ephesians 1:11; Hebrews 9:27).
- Human life is sacred (Psalm 139:13–16).
- Your life, including your body, belongs to God (1 Corinthians 6:13, 19; 1 Peter 4:1–2).

Dr. Ira Byock, a past president of the American Academy of Hospice and Palliative Medicine, says that the debate over physician-assisted suicide has diverted attention from more logical and humane solutions to a health crisis.

> Pain and other symptoms causing physical distress can be alleviated, even when they are severe. It is not always easy, but by being careful and comprehensive, and by being absolutely committed to do whatever is necessary to control physical distress, it can *always* be done. Personal suffering that derives from the experienced loss of meaning and from the feeling of impending disintegration can also be addressed. This, too, is not easy, but it can be done. How? One patient, one person, at a time.[9]

M. Scott Peck says, "I submit that the answer to the problem of assisted suicide lies not in more euthanasia, but in more hospice care. The first order of business should be to establish that dying patients have a constitutional right to competent hospice care."[10]

HOSPICE CARE

The sound of a vacuum cleaner rumbled above me as I ran from room to room in my parents' house, trying to put papers, dishes, and clothes in order. *She's coming home today,* I thought. Frantically trying to beat the clock, I checked on the cleaning lady's progress. I wanted everything to look perfect for my mom's arrival.

I glanced at my watch—still an hour before the scheduled delivery of a hospital bed, a bedside commode, and an IV pole. I wanted to have enough time to put on the sheets and organize all the other supplies before she came home.

Nursing is not a role in which I feel comfortable or competent. In the past, I had been the kind of hospital visitor who passed out when things got too scary. Needles, blood, procedures, and sick people made me feel very uneasy.

But Dad was the sole provider, and at a time before the Family Medical Leave Act, there was no way he could take a leave from his job. They needed an income in order to pay the medical bills. So as a family we decided that my sister and I would become Mom's primary caregivers, with my dad providing respite on weekends and evenings.

When I became a primary caregiver, I discovered something: With God's strength and the support of family, friends, clergy, and hospice, I *could* and *did* take care of my mother's physical needs. Monitoring my mom's pain medication, rinsing her stomach bag, and changing her was not fun and certainly not easy, but I found fulfillment and satisfaction in helping her. She was at home with us, and we faced death together with her. I couldn't imagine it being any other way.

I speak highly of hospice care based on our family's experience with it. After an acute hospitalization, Mom was under hospice care for less than a month. Looking back, I think it would have been better had she gone on it two months before her death, when she and her physician decided to discontinue all curative treatments. Of course, hindsight is always clearer.

> *It is still hard to believe that the pleasure of eating is over for good. This is still very hard to take. I am simply tired of the struggle and ready for this portion of my life to be over. But the goal now is to try to draw heaven into this life as much as possible. I am asking the Lord to give me the grace for this time and learn to recognize Him in the daily events.*

The first hospice program in the United States began serving patients in 1974. Within the past several years, the hospice movement has rapidly gained popularity, and as of September 2000, the NHPCO estimates that there are 3,139 operational or planned hospice programs in the United States, including the District of Columbia, Puerto Rico, and Guam. The NHPCO estimates that in 1999 hospices served at least 700,000 patients (or 29 percent of all Americans who died that year), up from 540,000 in 1998.[11]

According to NHPCO, hospice is not a particular place, but a philosophy of care. It is "a special kind of care designed to provide sensitivity and support for people in the final phase of a terminal illness. Hospice care seeks to enable patients to carry on an alert, pain-free life and to manage other symptoms so that their last days may be spent with dignity and quality at home or in a homelike setting."

Virginia F. Sendor and Patrice M. O'Connor define it this way:

Hospice care is comfort care incorporating palliative medicine, pain control, and symptom management. This care does not prolong the dying process, nor does it shorten life. However, survival often is prolonged through the patient becoming more comfortable. Comfort often enhances function and, by improving function of the patient, hospices often provide quality time for dying patients and their families.[12]

Joanne Morton believes that it is important for family members or friends to understand that hospice "isn't just about caring for the dying—it is helping terminally ill people live a life of quality and comfort in spite of their illness." This service is not only for the patient, she adds. It also helps the family cope while they care for their loved one.

Although hospice care is one of the best options available today to terminally ill patients, their families, and caregivers, a 1999 survey indicated that 80 percent of American respondents did not know the meaning of the term *hospice* and that more than 90 percent of Americans did not know that Medicare is one of the means by which hospice care is funded.[13]

In addition to a lack of information, denial often prevents people from using hospice care. Even if a patient is terminally ill, he or she may be still feeling physically okay. In such a case, it's hard to say, "I'm dying." It's much easier not to think about death until it becomes impossible to ignore. It's also hard to give up curative treatments. With today's medical technology and advancements, there always seems to be one more treatment, surgery, or medicine that a patient can try.

Research released by the NHPCO shows that 25 percent of Americans over the age of forty-five say that they would not bring up issues related to their parent's death—even if the parent had a terminal illness and less than six months to live.

The same research shows that 50 percent of Americans say they would rely on family and friends to carry out their wishes about end-of-life care but that 75 percent of Americans have never made those wishes clearly known. Karen A. Davie, president of NHPCO, says, "By sharing our wishes about end of life, we remove a heavy burden from our family and friends, who will not have to wonder if they are doing the right thing."[14]

The NHPCO suggests that family members who want to initiate discussions about end-of-life care with their loved one consider taking the following steps.[15]

- **Choose the setting.** Find a quiet, comfortable place free from distraction where you can hold a one-on-one conversation. The setting should be private, and the conversation should be planned in advance, not held on the spur of the moment.
- **Ask permission.** People cope with end-of-life issues in many ways. Asking permission to discuss this topic assures your loved one that you will respect his wishes and honor them. (Several openers could be: "I'd like to talk about how you would like to be cared for if you got really sick. Is that okay?" or "If you ever got really sick I would be afraid of not knowing the kind of care you would like. Could we talk about this now? I'd feel better if we did.")
- **Talk about it.** You have initiated this conversation because you love this person. Focus on your desire to help him maintain a full and happy life, even during difficult times. Allow your loved one to set the pace, and use nonverbal communication to offer support; for example, nod your head in agreement, hold your loved one's hand, or reach out to offer a hug or comforting touch.
- **Be a listener.** This is not a debate. Sometimes just having someone to talk to is a big help. Be sure to hear what the person is saying. Listen for wants or needs that your loved one expresses. Show empathy and respect by addressing these wants and needs in a truthful and open way.
- **Do your homework.** These end-of-life decisions are, without a doubt, hard to make. Talk with your medical-care team, your family, clergy, and approach every decision with prayer.

You don't want to wait until a major problem occurs and you have to make decisions quickly under pressure. Don't put off considering the possibility of hospice care.

DECIDING ON HOSPICE CARE

Jacquie Johnson's father, who was terminally ill with esophageal cancer, was admitted to a skilled nursing facility under hospice care during the last weeks of his life. Jacquie cannot say enough good things about the hospice experience.

"I remember how nice all the rooms were," Jacquie says, "and the hospice nurses really knew what they were doing and were great." Because they explained everything to her and gave her written information about the different stages her father would go through, they helped prepare Jacquie so that she, in turn, was able to comfort and reassure her father. "They were committed to upholding his dignity and his comfort, and they gave him value right to the end."

If you are contemplating hospice care, either for yourself or a loved one, the following questions and answers will help you evaluate whether or not it is right for you and your family.

• **When should a decision about entering a hospice program be made, and who should make it?**
At any time during a life-limiting illness, it's appropriate to discuss all of a patient's care options, including hospice. By law, the decision belongs to the patient. Understandably, most people are uncomfortable with the idea of stopping aggressive efforts to "beat" the disease. Hospice staff members are highly sensitive to these concerns and always available to discuss them with the patient and family.

• **Should I wait for our physician to raise the possibility of hospice, or should I raise it first?**
The patient and family should feel free to discuss hospice care at any

time with their physician, other health-care professionals, clergy, or friends.

• **What if our physician doesn't know about hospice?**
Most physicians know about hospice. If your physician wants more information, it is available from the National Council of Hospice Professionals Physician Section, medical societies, State Hospice Organizations, or NHPCO's Hospice Information Line (800) 658-8898. In addition, anyone can obtain information on hospice from the American Cancer Society, the American Association of Retired Persons, and the Social Security Administration.

• **Can a hospice patient who shows signs of recovery be returned to regular medical treatment?**
Certainly. If the patient's condition improves and the disease seems to be in remission, he can be discharged from hospice and return to aggressive therapy or go on about his daily life. If the discharged patient should need to return to hospice care later, Medicare and most private insurance will allow additional coverage for this purpose.

• **What does the hospice admission process involve?**
One of the first things the hospice program will do is contact the patient's physician to make sure that he agrees that hospice care is appropriate for the patient at that time. (Most hospices have medical staff available to help patients who have no physician.) The patient will be asked to sign consent and insurance forms. These are similar to the forms patients sign when they enter a hospital.

• **Is there any special equipment I need or change I have to make in my home before hospice care begins?**
Your hospice provider will assess your needs, recommend any equipment, and help make arrangements to obtain any necessary

equipment. Often the need for equipment is minimal at first and increases as the disease progresses. In general, hospice will assist in any way it can to make home care as convenient, clean, and safe as possible. The so-called "hospice election form" says that the patient understands that the care is palliative (that is, aimed at pain relief and symptom control) rather than curative. It also outlines the services available. The form Medicare patients sign also tells how electing the Medicare hospice benefit affects other Medicare coverage.

- **How many family members or friends does it take to care for a patient at home?**
There's no set number. One of the first things a hospice team does is prepare an individualized care plan that addresses, among other things, how much care the patient needs. Hospice staff members visit regularly and are always available to answer medical questions, provide support, and teach caregivers.

- **Must someone be with the patient at all times?**
In the early weeks of care, it's usually not necessary for someone to be with the patient all the time. Later, however, since one of the most common fears of patients is the fear of dying alone, hospice generally recommends that someone be there continuously. While family and friends do deliver most of the care, hospices provide volunteers to assist with errands and give primary caregivers a break and time away.

- **How difficult is caring for a dying loved one at home?**
It's never easy, and sometimes it can be quite hard. At the end of a long, progressive illness, nights especially can be very long, lonely, and scary. So, hospices have staff available around the clock to consult by phone with the family and make night visits if appropriate. Remember that hospice can also provide trained volunteers to give family members a break or provide companionship to the patient.

- **What specific assistance does hospice provide home-based patients?**

Hospice patients are cared for by a team of physicians, nurses, social workers, counselors, hospice certified nursing assistants, clergy, therapists, and volunteers. Each provides assistance based on his own area of expertise. In addition, hospices provide medications, supplies, equipment, hospital services related to the terminal illness, and additional helpers in the home, if and when needed.

- **Does hospice do anything to make death come sooner?**

Hospice neither hastens nor postpones dying. Just as doctors and midwives lend support and expertise during the time of childbirth, hospice provides its presence and specialized knowledge during the dying process.

- **Is caring for the patient at home the only place hospice care can be delivered?**

No. Although 90 percent of hospice patient time is spent in a personal residence, some patients live in nursing homes or hospice centers.

- **How does hospice "manage" pain?**

Hospice believes that both emotional and spiritual pain are just as real and in need of attention as physical pain, so it addresses each. Hospice nurses and doctors are up-to-date on the latest medications and devices for pain and symptom relief. In addition, physical and occupational therapists can help patients to be as mobile and self-sufficient as they wish, and they are often joined by specialists schooled in music therapy, art therapy, massage, and diet counseling. Finally, various counselors, including clergy, are available to assist family members as well as patients.

• **Will medications prevent the patient from being able to talk or know what's happening?**

Usually not. It is the goal of hospice to have the patient as pain free and alert as possible. By constantly consulting with the patient, hospices have been very successful in reaching this goal.

• **Is hospice affiliated with any religious organization?**

No. While some churches and religious groups have started hospices (sometimes in connection with their hospitals), these hospices serve a broad community and do not require patients to adhere to any particular set of beliefs.

• **Is hospice care covered by insurance?**

Hospice coverage is widely available. It is provided by Medicare nationwide, by Medicaid in forty-two states, and by most private insurance providers. To be sure of coverage, families should, of course, check with their employers or health insurance providers.

• **If the patient is not covered by Medicare or any other health insurance, will hospice still provide care?**

The first thing hospice will do is assist families in finding out whether the patient is eligible for coverage that they may not be aware of. If there is no coverage, most hospices will provide for anyone who cannot pay by using money raised from the community or from memorial or foundation gifts.

• **Does hospice provide any help to the family after the patient dies?**

Hospice provides continuing contact and support for caregivers for at least a year after the death of a loved one. Most hospices also sponsor bereavement groups and support for anyone in the community who has experienced a death of a family member, a friend, or similar losses.

I think I have a partial answer to the loss of the enjoyment of food. The Lord has taken from me little by little the delights which I had continually enjoyed here. Gone is my strength, my sexuality, my job, my recreation (racquetball, etc.), and now my food. He wants me to see that I can find delight in Him alone. Each day I have been trying to turn to Him for my daily sustenance. Today we enjoyed a most enjoyable afternoon lying outside in a most perfect temperature. Isn't that what the Lord wants of us?

F

A CHECKLIST FOR MAKING END-OF-LIFE DECISIONS [16]

Information to gather

- ____ Diagnosis
- ____ Treatment options
- ____ Benefits versus risks (including side effects)
- ____ Treatment recommendations of attending physician
- ____ Additional medical consultation(s)
- ____ Prognosis (likely outcome)
- ____ Costs and resources
- ____ Time frame for reaching decision (urgency)

Factors to consider

- ____ Patient's wishes (including advance directives such as a living will or durable power of attorney)
- ____ Expectations of patients and/or family
- ____ Patient's relationship with God
- ____ Patient's reconciliation with family/friends
- ____ Costs and resources

Principles involved

 ____ Principle of medical ethics
 ____ Principle of biblical ethics
 ____ Specific biblical texts

Acceptable options/directions

 ____ Acceptable by secular standards
 ____ Acceptable by biblical standards
 ____ Acceptable to patient/surrogate
 ____ Acceptable to family
 ____ Acceptable to church support system

Resources

 ____ Medical consultant
 ____ Ethics committee or consultant
 ____ Family support (emotional/spiritual/economic)
 ____ Spiritual (pastor/church)
 ____ Social services
 ____ Psychological
 ____ Financial
 ____ Other agencies, such as hospice

There is an appointed time for everything.
And there is a time for every event under heaven—
A time to give birth, and a time to die...
A time to weep, and a time to laugh,
A time to mourn, and a time to dance.

ECCLESIASTES 3:1–2, 4

———◦◦◦———

F
I looked out over Jordan, and what did I see,
Coming for to carry me home?
A band of angels coming after me,
Coming for to carry me home.

AUTHOR UNKNOWN

Ten

Letting Go

"Oh, these are gorgeous," Rebecca said, turning toward me. "Which one do you want?" She held up a cameo and a Venetian glass bead necklace with a matching bracelet. I liked both of them, but the vibrant colors especially appealed to me. "I think I'd like the necklace," I replied.

"Your father bought those for me when he was traveling in Italy in 1976," my mom said. She was lying in bed with an open jewelry box. "He told me that they would look beautiful on me." Her face was flushed, warmed by the memory.

For two hours, Mom sorted through her jewelry. As she handed each item to us and told us the story behind it, my sister and I found joy in our family's history.

Unlike sudden death, when there is no chance for good-byes, terminal illness allows friends and family an incredible opportunity—a last, and perhaps life-changing chance—to relive cherished moments, give or receive forgiveness, resolve conflict, and voice important thoughts and concerns.

Acknowledging Death

When he was a teenager, a friend of mine lost his mother. His family didn't discuss problems, so it didn't surprise him that there was no open communication when his mother became ill. "I didn't find out that my mom was dying until I overheard my dad telling someone over the phone," he says. "The way my family dealt with things was to not talk about them."

When his mother went to the hospital for the last time, he was unable to go. This had a negative effect on my friend's ability to cope with his mother's death. "I really think it would have helped me if I had been there and had also taken opportunities to talk with her earlier about her heritage, about the future, and about her dying," he says.

Terminally ill patients and their families often end up playing a game of "let's pretend." Everyone knows what's going on but pretends that the patient will eventually get better. People who play that game, however, eventually admit that their loved ones knew that they were dying, despite everyone's pretenses.

Saying good-bye is an important part of dying, according to Rev. Joseph Nilsen. But, he says, "I frequently find spouses and children who can't or won't let go or give their loved one permission to die." Robert Kastenbaum says that it's much harder for people to say good-bye if they do not realize or do not want to acknowledge that they are dying.[1] Nonacceptance, in turn, can keep the emotional, physical, and spiritual needs of both the patient and family from being met during the final phase of a patient's life.

For most people, acknowledging and accepting death is one of the most critical components of dying well. While I was interviewing people for this book, the most common statement I heard from those who had lost a loved one to a terminal illness was "I wish we could have talked together about his death." Many family members harbor regrets that range from a loss of family history to a lack of closure in the relationship. Talking openly about my mom's death with her and other family members made it more bearable for me, both before and after her death.

Some semblance of acceptance has settled on me.

Dr. Stuart Roop believes that communication and honesty are crucial for the patient and the family. "Some families believe that they are helping their loved ones by protecting them from the truth, and they might even ask a doctor not to tell a patient the news," he says. He tells them that he cannot lie if their loved one asks him about his condition. Unless there are extreme circumstances, he encourages resistant family members to talk with their loved one about what is happening. If they don't, he says, "Families will look back on this situation and replay it over and over again in their minds, asking themselves, 'Did I do the right thing?'" On the other hand, most families who have discussed things with their loved ones don't second-guess their decisions.[2]

Roop also believes that in the long run it is much better for patients to know, so they can be involved in making end-of-life decisions. The authors of *Fading Away* agree. "When patients use specific strategies for preparing for death, communicate openly about their wishes, and attend to details surrounding the death and afterwards, they have a sense of completion and satisfaction. They have done the best they can to make it as easy as possible for family members."[3]

The importance of planning and discussing wishes *ahead of time* cannot be overemphasized. This includes even the most specific details of care. I remember when we asked a home-health aide to come bathe my mom. Unfortunately, we did not know that it would really bother her. After the aide left, she was crying and upset. She told me that it made her feel as though her family had abandoned her. We felt terrible and only wished we had known this beforehand.

Even though I am ready to go, I am sad to leave my family.

One of the primary objectives of hospice care is to "maintain open, direct, and honest communication with the terminally ill person and his or her family."[4] The many conversations we had with my mom's hospice nurses were reassuring because we didn't have to read between the lines or try to figure out what they meant. They compassionately laid out all the facts and encouraged us to ask questions. That gave us something to discuss when we were alone, so we could make decisions together. Even though my mom made almost all the decisions about her end-of-life care, she seemed to take comfort in discussing her choices with us.

Here are some ways you can acknowledge and prepare for an impending death.

As a patient, you can:

- Talk about your death with your family and friends.
- Plan your funeral or memorial service with your spouse, your children, a close friend, or clergy. If you have specific requests, let your family know. My mom, for example, did not want to have a viewing or a casket at the memorial service.
- Make a list of people you want the family to contact upon your death. You may want to arrange a pyramid-type calling list. My mom asked her sisters to call that side of the family and a former coworker to contact her colleagues at work.
- Make sure that your will is in order, and, if you feel like it, distribute any special possessions.

As a family member or friend, you can:

- Be willing to talk about death and the future with your loved one, even if it's painful.
- Reassure your loved one that you will carry out his specific wishes with regard to the funeral and the disposition of his remains.

- Prepare yourself: Get counseling, talk with friends, and find the support you need.
- Be there with your loved one. Talk, sing, pray, read, or just sit.

The daily challenge is not to give up—not to anticipate death. I must continually praise the Lord for all the blessings He has bestowed upon me and recognize that life is today—not tomorrow. Never tomorrow.

SAYING GOOD-BYE

Once you know that your time is limited, you may not know what to say or do. This is normal. Your family and friends probably don't know what to say or do, either. You can set whatever tone you wish within your circle of support. If you have chosen to be open and honest about your death, you can purposefully choose how to say good-bye to those who mean the most to you.

Words, written and spoken, can provide a powerful means of closure. I cannot remember the last words my mom said before she slipped into a coma, approximately forty-eight hours before her death. Fortunately, we had enjoyed hours of conversation during the previous month. I had been able to share everything I wanted to say to her, and so had she.

In a letter my mom left for me to read after she died, she says:

I'm sorry that I started this so late for I will not be able to finish it. You know that I love you very much and wish that we had many more years than we have had. I look forward to you joining me some day in the future. Do not cry for me for I am in the best place…. Know that I love you very much and am sorry that I have to leave your life so soon.

This letter is very precious to me. I believe that Mom felt a peace about leaving words for me to read later. I also wrote to her before she died. In a letter and a poem, I told her how much she had affected my life. I wanted her to know, without any doubt, how much she meant to me.

When talking with dying patients and their families, be very sensitive to their dignity and treat them with great respect, advises Rev. Harold A. Peeders.[5] He says that there are several invaluable things that the family of a dying person can do at the end of their loved one's life.

- Say, **"Please forgive me"** and **"I forgive you."** A pastor might help facilitate this wonderful gift of forgiveness.
- Say, **"Thanks for everything."** This is a statement of celebration. Sometimes people can be more specific, but it is an incredible thing for a patient to hear this.
- Say, **"I love you."** Verbalizing your love is extremely important.
- Say, **"Good-bye."** Articulating this can allow for healing and closure.

"If possible before your loved one dies, talk about past problems and future plans—anything you wish you'd talked about," recommends Jane Phung, whose mother-in-law died of liver failure. "Try to have no regrets. Give hugs, touch each other, listen to each other, enjoy each moment, cry together a little, laugh together a lot, forgive each other, speak of your faith, of God, and of the future."

Elizabeth Harris spent as much time as possible with her mother, who was dying of ovarian cancer. "The nurses in the hospital were very accommodating," she remembers. "They kept the bed in her room empty so that I could sleep there. Having that privilege made it easier for me to comfort her and keep her comfortable." Harris points out that being able to do things for her mother was comforting to her as well as her mother. "I felt like I was ministering to her," she says.

Saying good-bye can take a variety of forms, depending on your likes, dislikes, personality, sharing style, and family dynamics. Here are a few ideas about how to say good-bye.

As a patient, you can:

- Evaluate your life and accomplishments and feel good about them. "What have I done that is important? How have I made a difference in someone's life? What is one choice or decision I feel really good about having made in my lifetime?"
- Look through family photo albums, watch a slide show of old vacation slides, or view old movies.
- Human life is sacred (Psalm 139:13–16).
- Work on a special project (alone or with your family) or family history (a video, an audiotape, etc.) to leave as a legacy.
- Give away a possession that has significance for the one to whom you give it.
- Do something together (celebrate a birthday, anniversary, or other milestone), or, if possible, go somewhere together (attend church one last time, visit a favorite park, see a movie, or eat at a favorite restaurant).
- Make phone calls or write letters to long-distance relatives and friends to tell them good-bye and express your appreciation of them.
- Write a letter to your family or other special people in your life for them to read after your death.
- Talk to your spouse about the future without you.
- Don't be afraid to speak up and ask for private time with your spouse, a sibling, children, or a friend.
- Reminisce together, and feel thankful and grateful for those memories.

As a family member or friend, you can:

- Write a letter expressing your love and appreciation for your loved one. Several of my mom's friends who lived far away wrote letters of good-bye. Their words shared what they liked so much about her, told her what they would miss about her, and painted pictures of where she was going.

- Say how you plan to include your loved one in your life, even after he is gone (name a child or grandchild after him, do something he has always wanted you to do, etc.)

- Be sensitive to your loved one's wish for privacy, either to have some alone time or to spend time with a spouse. He may not want to hurt your feelings.

- Resolve any conflicts.

CROSSING THE RIVER

Together, the medical-care team, clergy, family members, and friends can address the patient's needs—psychological, emotional, relational, and spiritual as well as physical. Hospice and palliative-care workers are trained to help you and your family deal with any potential problem or fear.

If, as a caregiver, you have specific concerns about alleviating distress or discomfort in your loved one, always check with the physician, nurse, or palliative-care team. Joanne Morton offers a few general suggestions to keep in mind as you provide continuous care for your loved one.

- Keep blankets on him to prevent him from feeling too cold; however, do not use electric blankets.

- Plan to talk with him at the times when he is most alert.

- Elevate the head of the bed often to relieve irregular breathing patterns.

- If he is confused, talk calmly and assuredly in order not to startle or frighten him further.

- Remind him frequently what day it is, what time it is, and who is in the room talking with him.

- If he is incontinent, buy pads to place under him. (Consult your nurse.)
- Provide a cool mist humidifier to increase the humidity in the room.
- Change his position, keeping him off of his back.
- Provide ice chips, a straw, and cool, moist washcloths to relieve feelings of dehydration. (Your nurse will show you how to use mouth swabs and Vaseline to relieve dryness of the lips and mouth.)
- Keep a light on in the room when his vision decreases (if it is okay with him).
- Always assume that he can hear you.

Clergy are an excellent source of spiritual and emotional support for dying patients and their families. Peeders and Nilsen both offer the comfort of prayer and touch to dying patients. In most visitations, Peeders asks permission to lay hands on a patient's shoulders or head while he prays. "Laying hands on an individual in prayer is a powerful thing," he says. "I also encourage the person to pray with me—as we pray the Lord's Prayer, together."

"If I am there [when a person has just died]," says Nilsen, "I try to have everyone hold hands around the bedside, and I commend the person to the Lord." Giving Holy Communion to a dying patient is another sacramental way Peeders shows care and concern for those who have grown up with this tradition and are involved in a community of faith.

Family members can read favorite verses to their loved one and offer prayers of comfort, peace, and strength. My mom loved for us to read Psalms and verses that referred to heaven and to God's comfort and love.

Lori read to me from the Scriptures. From that I gained more peace than through any other means that day.

What do people fear most about dying? It is difficult to predict the psychological state and needs of a dying patient because people differ according to age, cultural background, education, and socio-economic status. Nevertheless, certain fears recur frequently.[6]

According to psychotherapist Joanne Morton, the ten most common fears of death are:

dying alone;
pain or discomfort;
losing control over one's body;
losing one's loved ones;
being completely helpless and/or dependent;
dying suddenly or violently (hemorrhage);
dying before one is ready to go;
abandoning those who need you;
death being the end of feeling/thinking;
not having time to make amends.

I live in a different world from everyone else. This world set apart—my goals are different, my hopes are different. Dave goes off to work among the living. I stay home to die among dead things. I have already died many times and I probably will die many times more before I actually leave this earth. No matter how many are around you, you still die alone.

Unfortunately, American culture leads many to believe that dying is a horrible aspect of family life, "a crisis only to be endured." Yet the end of life is an important time, for that is when patients take stock of what they have been, say important farewells to loved ones, provide final guidance and advice for family affairs, and find meaning in their lives.[7] Dr. Ira Byock puts it this way: "When the human dimension of dying is nurtured, for many the transition from life can become as profound, intimate, and precious as the miracle of birth."[8]

Then I thought how I am possibly only weeks away from death now. How can things feel so normal and yet be drawing to an end? What new sounds will there be in the next life? Will I be aware of this passage? Can I watch the translation from time to eternity take place? What will I remember of this life?

In the classic allegory *Pilgrim's Progress,* John Bunyan describes the pilgrim, Standfast, crossing the river into the Celestial City:

"This River makes so many afraid!" said he; "indeed, I was frightened myself before I entered it. But my fear is all gone; I can feel the firm ground under my feet, and very soon I shall be with my Prince. It has been very pleasant to hear of Him and think of Him, but now I shall see Him with my own eyes. He has helped me and strengthened me all through my pilgrimage, and He is with me now."[9]

May you feel the firm ground beneath you when you cross the river!

Am I afraid to look forward to heaven for the same reason I have always been afraid to look forward to anything on earth, that I will be disappointed by not getting to go or it does not turn out to meet my expectations?

F

PEACE AT THE BEDSIDE

Most everyone will have fears or doubts (some expressed and some unexpressed) about death or the events leading up to it. The following list gives biblically based promises to help you conquer your fear of death.

- Jesus will not forsake you, even at death (Psalm 23:4; Hosea 13:14).
- God is always faithful (Psalm 36:5; 89:24; 119:90; Lamentations 3:23; 1 Corinthians 1:9; 2 Thessalonians 5:24).
- God will give you strength to endure whatever may come upon you (Psalm 37:24; 1 Corinthians 10:13; Philippians 4:13).
- Though you walk in the midst of trouble, God will take care of you (Psalm 138:7).
- God will swallow up death for all time (Isaiah 25:8).
- God will wipe away every tear from your eyes (Isaiah 25:8; Revelation 21:4).
- Christians have the assurance of salvation and eternal life in heaven (John 3:16; Romans 10:9).
- God has prepared a place for you in heaven (John 14:2–3).
- Present sufferings are not worthy to be compared with the glory that is to be revealed to you (Romans 8:18).
- Death will never separate you from God's love (Romans 8:38–39).
- Jesus has conquered death through the Resurrection (1 Corinthians 15:26; 2 Timothy 1:10).

"In My Father's house are many dwelling places;
if it were not so, I would have told you;
for I go to prepare a place for you.
And if I go and prepare a place for you,
I will come again,
and receive you to Myself;
that where I am, there you may be also."

JOHN 14:2–3

F
For though from out our bourne of Time and Place
The flood may bear me far,
I hope to see my Pilot face to face
When I have crossed the bar.

ALFRED LORD TENNYSON

Eleven

A Journey of Hope

Too weak to stand or even sit up, my mother was confined to bed the last few days of her life. One of us was always with her, day and night. We spent time talking, singing, praying, listening to Christian or classical music, and reading the Bible to her. We sat or snuggled as close as we could without making her uncomfortable. Her emaciated face only accentuated the sparkle in her blue eyes.

Heaven was a popular topic of conversation. Mom often talked about what she was looking forward to after she died. She encouraged us not to be too sad at her early departure because of where she was going and with whom she would be. As we imagined the heavenly residence she was about to enter, our tears of sorrow and frustration melted into smiles and laughter.

"Just think of the host of angels that will rejoice when I finally attain my completeness in Christ," Mom said. "No more pain, no more cancer, and no more death—only perfect and glory-filled fellowship with God."

Believing that you will spend eternity in heaven affects both your perspective of death and your life on earth. "Faith is double-sided," says Joni Eareckson Tada. "It not only verifies heaven as real, giving hard and fast reality to that which we do not see, but it also makes us look differently at visible things on earth. Through faith's eyes, heaven becomes a rock-solid home, and the concrete world in which we live becomes drained of substance and importance."[1]

GOING HOME

On Tuesday, September 6, 1994, I maneuvered around the IV line and carefully climbed into my mom's rented hospital bed. I settled in close to her body and read a book, without really reading it. Our heads were on the same pillow. The closeness was comforting.

The only sound in the room was her breathing, fast and forced but in a rhythm. Then I noticed a gap, a space between her breaths. I put down my book and held her hand. Her fingernails were blue. Then I caressed her face and stroked her hair.

"I love you, Mom—I always will," I whispered. "Are you feeling okay? Do you have pain anywhere?"

The nurses had shown us how to give her extra doses of morphine from the pump when we sensed her discomfort. Her guardians against pain, we watched her constantly. Through the hospice team, pain medication, and God's grace, her pain had remained under control.

I sensed something was different this time, and I urged my sister to come quickly. Rebecca hurried up the stairs and into the bedroom. "See?" I asked, nearly choking on the question. "Don't you think her breathing is becoming more labored, like the nurses said it would?"

She, too, climbed into bed. For several minutes we talked with my mom and reassured her that everything was going to be okay. Slowly, our words became prayers. We prayed for God to ease her transition from death to life. We thanked God for her. We asked for His mercy. We prayed for comfort.

One gasp…and another. Then…silence.

At 3:55 P.M. my mother entered the kingdom of heaven. Rebecca and I cried and held her between us for one last time. Rebecca's eyes literally shone through her tears. "But, Lori, it's so wonderful because she's in heaven now," she said. After everything Mom had endured in her earthly body for four and a half years, she was with God, rejoicing in heaven. She was finally home.

There is a huge difference in the outlook of those who believe they are going to heaven after they die and those who believe that all existence stops at the grave. Believing that my mom was headed for heaven, I accepted her dying better. Though I ached for her physical presence to continue, I knew that she would be free from pain and that someday we would be reunited in God's holy presence.

This earthly life is filled with sorrow and pain. It only makes sense if there is something to look forward to. Whatever pain or misery awaits me before I die, I can endure it because I know that God will use it to help perfect me and prepare me for dwelling in heaven. I desire my life to bring glory to God.

If heaven is your real home, what is it like?

In his booklet *Heaven,* Joseph Bayly says that death is "deliverance to life beyond your imagining. The death incident is merely a passage from earth life, from the womb that has contained you until now, into the marvelous newness of heaven life. You'll go through a dark tunnel; you may experience pain—just as you did when you were born a baby—but beyond the tunnel is heaven. I promise you, you'll enjoy heaven."[2]

For centuries, mystery has shrouded much of the discussion about heaven, because we can't talk about it in an empirical sense. I try not to get wrapped up in the specifics of heaven and just concentrate on what the Bible says about it. Many verses throughout the Old and New Testaments describe what heaven will be like and what we as redeemed saints will experience there.

Heaven is a place with many wonderful, hard-to-imagine qualities.

Heaven is holy (Deuteronomy 26:15; Psalm 20:6; Isaiah 57:15); a paradise (2 Corinthians 12:2, 4); a rest (Hebrews 4:9); everlasting (Psalm 89:29; 2 Corinthians 5:1); immeasurable (Jeremiah 31:37); beautiful (Revelation 4:1–6; 21:10–21; 22:1–5); and new (Revelation 21:2, 5).

Heaven is the place where God dwells.

Right now God is reigning supreme over everything in heaven and earth from His throne, which He created (Nehemiah 9:6; Psalm 135:6). The Lord said to the prophet Isaiah, "Heaven is My throne and the earth is My footstool" (Isaiah 66:1; also Acts 7:49), and Moses asked God to "Look down from Thy holy habitation, from heaven, and bless Thy people Israel" (Deuteronomy 26:15). The Lord's Prayer also says where God is: "Our Father who art in heaven" (Matthew 6:9). See also Genesis 28:17; 1 Kings 8:30; Psalm 11:4; and Psalm 80:14.

Heaven is the place where good angels dwell.

When Jesus told His disciples about His return to earth in glory, He said that no one, "not even the angels of heaven," would know the exact time it would take place, except God, the Father (Matthew 24:36). In his vision, the prophet Isaiah saw seraphim with God (Isaiah 6:2); and in his, Ezekiel saw four living beings (Ezekiel 1:5–6). There is a similar description in Revelation 4:6–9.

Heaven is where we will reign with Christ.

We will be busy working and completing fulfilling, satisfying tasks (Isaiah 65:21–23). The most incredible of these heavenly activities will be reigning forever with Christ (2 Timothy 2:12; Revelation 3:21; 22:5), which includes judging angels (1 Corinthians 6:3). We will see Jesus face-to-face and worship God eternally (Revelation

7:9–15). His name will be on our foreheads (Revelation 22:4).

Heaven is the place where we will receive our inheritance and reward.

All the saints will have their names recorded in heaven (Luke 10:20; Hebrews 12:23).

Those who have laid up treasures in heaven will receive what they have stored there (Matthew 6:20; Luke 12:33). We also have an inheritance waiting for us (Ephesians 1:11; 1 Peter 1:4).

Heaven is a place where we will be eternally well and happy.

After death we will be transformed into Christ's likeness (1 John 3:2). We will have new, immortal bodies that will never wear out or get sick (1 Corinthians 15:42–44), and we will never again experience pain or sorrow. "He shall wipe away every tear from their eyes; and there shall no longer be any death; there shall no longer be any mourning, or crying, or pain" (Isaiah 65:19–20; Revelation 21:4).

> I truly am anticipating meeting Him. From what I know of heaven, it is going to be wonderful there.
> *No more sorrow or pain.
> *Real fellowship with Christians from all time. I look forward to talking with: C. S. Lewis, Paul, John Bunyan, and many people I have read about through the ages.
> *Fellowship with Jesus (I suspect all questions will be answered).
> *Life in the eternal city.
> *Fruitful, fulfilling work.

We have a truly incredible future waiting just beyond death's door. Rest in the comfort of heaven's reality.

GETTING THERE

Heaven is where most people want to go after they die, and it's comforting to believe that *all* people go there. However, Jesus made it clear that not all people do: "Not everyone who says to Me, 'Lord, Lord,' will enter the kingdom of heaven" (Matthew 7:21–23). He also said, "I am the way, and the truth, and the life; no one comes to the Father, but through Me" (John 14:6).

Ultimately every person will face God's judgment (Romans 14:10, 12; Hebrews 9:27; 1 Peter 4:5). God's standard for judgment is perfection, yet no one is perfect. That's why God sent His only Son—to pay for our sins so that we can stand in His presence. God never would have sacrificed His Son if He were willing to overlook sin and let us into heaven anyway. Physical death is inevitable, and there are only two ways to die—in faith or in sin. Therefore, as Billy Graham says, "There is no more urgent and critical question in life than that of your personal relationship with God and your eternal salvation."[3]

Yet, we are not cast adrift to figure it all out on our own. There are clues given to us by God. First, there was the example of the Israelites, who were shown in a rather pointed fashion that they were unable to produce a good life doing things their way. Then God sent Jesus Christ to be the vehicle of salvation for all men, not just the Jews. At the same time, He showed mankind just what a God-centered life looks like so that others could emulate Him. Finally, we are given the written word of God so that we can study and understand the instructions God has given.

What about the other religions, one might ask? Each one of them has a kernel of truth also found in Christianity, but none of them has the way of salvation.

There was only one Jesus and it was through His sacrifice, the sacrifice accepted by God as evidenced by the resurrection, that we could come to God without our sins blocking the approach.

Your illness offers a special opportunity for you, your family, and your friends to evaluate your lives and what lies ahead. Do you know what will happen to you when you die? Will you die in faith or in sin?

No matter how good you consider yourself, you can never meet God's standard of holiness. Picture yourself on one side of a wide, deep canyon. God is on one side, and you're on the other. You've spent a long time preparing for your final leap across to reach Him. You've done all the right things in life and even attended church and prayed. True, you may be able to leap farther than someone else, but your own efforts just aren't enough to carry you all the way. The divide is too vast! But there is a toll-free bridge that you can take, and it's in the shape of a cross.[4]

How do you die in faith? *To die in faith you must first live in faith.* It does not matter how long your faithful life lasts. It could be one second, or it could span decades. You live in faith by choice. It's your decision and yours alone. All you have to do is:

- **Acknowledge that you are a sinner.** "For all have sinned and fall short of the glory of God" (Romans 3:23). "If we say that we have no sin, we are deceiving ourselves, and the truth is not in us.... If we say that we have not sinned, we make Him a liar, and His word is not in us" (1 John 1:8, 10).
- **Repent of your sins to God and ask for His forgiveness.** "If we confess our sins, He is faithful and righteous to forgive us our sins and to cleanse us from all unrighteousness" (1 John 1:9).

- **Trust in Jesus Christ as your personal Savior for your salvation.** "For God so loved the world, that He gave His only begotten Son, that whoever believes in Him should not perish, but have eternal life" (John 3:16).

You can make this decision by praying a simple prayer right now.

Dear heavenly Father,

I know that I am a sinner, and I need You. I need Your forgiveness. Please forgive me. I believe that You sent Your only Son, Jesus, to die on the cross for all my sins—past, present, and future. I believe that He rose again from the dead so I could be saved and live with You forever in heaven. I invite You to come into my life right now as my personal Savior. I trust You and promise to follow You as Lord of my life.

In Jesus' name, amen.

If you prayed this prayer for the first time, you are now a beloved child of God. You have passed out of death into life (John 5:24). Through God's grace, your sins have been forgiven, and you've received the gift of eternal life (Ephesians 2:8). Angels are celebrating in heaven at this very moment (Luke 15:10).

GETTING READY

Even though your salvation and entrance into heaven are based only upon your faith and acceptance of what God has already done for you, it's wise to evaluate what you are doing and focusing on during your earthly stay. A terminal illness is an excellent opportunity for family members and friends to reconsider the paths they have chosen. Time is too precious to throw away without thinking carefully about who you are and where you are going. Have you been seeking God's kingdom and building treasures in heaven, or have you devoted your time and energy to storing up earthly wealth that is perishable?

Ultimately, God will judge what you have done on earth. That's what the apostle Paul told the Corinthians:

> Each man's work will become evident; for the day will show it, because it is to be revealed with fire; and the fire itself will test the quality of each man's work. If any man's work which he has built upon it remains, he shall receive a reward. If any man's work is burned up, he shall suffer loss; but he himself shall be saved, yet so as through fire. (1 Corinthians 3:13–15)

When you are near a loved one who is standing at the very edge of eternity, it is much easier to see which of your past actions, thoughts, and decisions had lasting value and importance. I want to make sure that my works, which have first been built on the foundation laid by Jesus, are not burned up because they were worthless wood, hay, and straw. I want to make sure that my actions, choices, values, relationships, and thoughts all line up with seeking God's kingdom and righteousness. I want to do things that have value for eternity and are being laid up as treasures in heaven (see Matthew 6:19–24, 33–34; 19:21).

No matter how we have lived our lives, God will extend His grace if we ask. His greatest desire is for everyone to believe in Jesus and have eternal life (John 6:40). If you are feeling unsure about your salvation because of your past, read the words Jesus spoke to the thief hanging on the cross next to Him: "Truly I say to you, today you shall be with Me in Paradise" (Luke 23:43). God promises that "if you confess with your mouth 'Jesus is Lord,' and believe in your heart that God raised Him from the dead, you will be saved" (Romans 10:9, NIV).

When Jacquie Johnson's father was dying of esophageal cancer, she was very afraid that he was not going to make a commitment to Christ. "I felt like I was a failure and didn't do what I should have done," said Jacquie, who prayed for another opportunity. "I really wanted to know without a shadow of a doubt that he heard and understood me."

Jacquie prepared in advance for their conversation, hoping she wouldn't freeze or forget what to say. "I journaled about what I should say and how I should say it, and then I practiced out loud while I was driving in my car," she said.

Finally Jacquie broached the topic with her father. "Dad, I know we've talked about this before, but I need to know if you've made your peace with God," she said. She remembers telling him the New Testament parable about the farmer who hired some workers at the beginning of the day, promised them a certain wage, and then hired additional workers at the end and promised them the same amount of money. "The whole point of that story is that God doesn't care when you come to Him. No matter what has happened in life, He will give you the same right to enter heaven as someone who has been a Christian his entire life.

"If I could trade places with you right now to let you know how important it is to me for you to have a relationship with God, I would do it," Jacquie continued. "I want more than anything to know that I will see you in heaven." At that point, she says, her father began crying, and she knew that he had heard and understood what she said. "I felt a peace because I knew that he realized how much I loved him."

I began to think about why I was here in the first place. I never had any exalted idea that I was anything unusual. I would never go down in history books as someone who did anything to be remembered. The best I would be remembered for was that I had done a pretty good job as a mother and wife. Surely, life had to have more of a goal than that. We were not poor, nor were we rich. Actually, we had never been without anything we needed, yet many people had much more and could travel to exotic places and do fun things, which we could never afford. Had I missed out on life because I hadn't had the money to do fun things? Are we on this earth to have fun?

As these thoughts took shape, I began to realize that it was a pretty poor world if we were here to simply have fun. So much of everyone's life is consumed with work; some never have anything because of great poverty and rotten political situations. Some people have severe disabilities, which keep them from living a full life. Are these people destined to have an unfulfilling life because of things that they never could control? If this were true, then there is no God in heaven. If there is a loving God, there must be a reason for each of us to be here and the potential for every one of us to live a fulfilled life.

As I looked at the Scriptures, I found that in every case, the focus was away from the physical world around us. We are never encouraged to involve ourselves so much in the physical that we neglect the more important spiritual side of life. Consistently, we are encouraged to give things away, not expecting them back; distrust riches; seek God's kingdom and not worry about food or clothing; be the salt of the earth by your good works; and cultivate a thankful attitude for everything that happens. The moment we become too focused on ourselves, whether it be on our health, our beauty, our activities, or our honor, we have missed the point of why we are here on earth.

I found the peace I was seeking once I laid aside the attitudes of my culture and accepted the control of God over all of my life. I discovered that my real illness is not the cancer which affects only my mortal body, but rather is the subtle inclusion in my life of all the desire for my rights, my life, my honor, and wealth, power, and prestige. The cancer will disappear when I die and I will enjoy an eternity of love and joy with no more sorrow.

Multnomah Publishers

The publisher and author would love to hear your comments about this book. *Please contact us at:*
www.multnomah.net/findinghope

A Letter of Encouragement

Dear Reader,

The road you may be traveling is, without a doubt, difficult. The bumps, potholes, and rocks are hard to avoid. Sometimes dust can get in your eyes, making it difficult to see and think clearly. You probably feel tired, overwhelmed, and possibly alone.

We pray that you experience and feel God's love, strength, and peace along the way. He will provide everything you need, when you need it, one step at a time. He holds you in the palm of His hand and will protect and care for you. Nothing is allowed to touch you except with His permission—and even then, He will carefully control all circumstances so that you are "afflicted in every way, but not crushed; perplexed, but not despairing; persecuted, but not forsaken; struck down, but not destroyed" (2 Corinthians 4:8–9).

Remember your treasure! God has promised that you have a treasure in your earthly body, which is the "surpassing greatness of the power of God" (2 Corinthians 4:7). Live each day off of His power instead of your own.

A word of encouragement for family members and close friends: Remember your loved one's salvation is not totally dependent upon you and your efforts to witness to him. You aren't in charge of changing hearts; God's Spirit is.

We consider it a privilege to have walked alongside you for a little while on your journey. We hope that our words have been encouraging and comforting to you as we have pointed you toward our own source of Hope—God Himself.

> "'The LORD bless you, and keep you; The LORD make His face shine upon you, and be gracious to you; The LORD lift up His countenance on you, and give you peace.'" (Numbers 6:24–26)

In Christ's love and strength,

Laurel S. Brunvoll

David G. Seiler

P.S. We would love to hear from you! Please contact us at:
brunvoll@erols.com
dseiler@starpower.net

A Topical List of Encouraging Bible Verses and Hymns

The following list of Bible verses and hymns is arranged topically to help you find a specific verse or hymn that will meet you where you are and encourage your soul during your time of need.

Anger

Psalm 37:8; Proverbs 14:17, 29; 16:32; 29:11; Ecclesiastes 7:9; Ephesians 4:31–32; Colossians 3:8; James 1:19–20

Anxiety and Worry

Psalm 55:22; Matthew 6:33–34; Philippians 4:6–7; 1 Peter 5:7

"O God, Our Help in Ages Past" by Isaac Watts (1674–1748)

O God, our help in ages past, Our hope for years to come, Our shelter from the stormy blast, And our eternal home!/Under the shadow of Thy throne, Still may we dwell secure; Sufficient is Thine arm alone, And our defense is sure./Before the hills in order stood, Or earth received her frame, From everlasting Thou art God, To endless years the same./Time, like an ever-rolling stream, Bears all its sons away; They fly forgotten as a dream, Dies at the o-p'ning day./O God, our help in ages past, Our hope for years to come, Be Thou our guide while life shall last, And our eternal home.

BEREAVEMENT

2 Samuel 12:23; Psalm 23:4, 6; John 11:25; 14:1–3; 1 Corinthians 13:12; 2 Corinthians 5:1; Philippians 1:21; 1 Peter 1:3–4

"I'll Praise My Maker While I've Breath" by Isaac Watts (1674–1748)

I'll praise my Maker while I've breath; And when my voice is lost in death, Praise shall employ my nobler pow'rs; My days of praise shall ne'er be past, While life, and thought, and being last, Or immortality endures. Happy the man whose hopes rely On Israel's God! He made the sky, And earth, and sea, with all their train: His truth forever stands secure; He saves the oppressed, He feeds the poor, And none shall find His promise vain. The Lord gives eyesight to the blind; The Lord supports the fainting mind; He sends the laboring conscience peace; He helps the stranger in distress, The widow and fatherless And grants the prisoner sweet release. I'll praise Him while He lends me breath; And when my voice is lost in death, Praise shall employ my nobler pow'rs; My days of praise shall ne'er be past, While life, and thought, and being last, Or immortality endures.

BEREAVEMENT: DEALING WITH GRIEF

Isaiah 43:2; Matthew 5:4; 2 Corinthians 1:3–5, 9; 2 Timothy 1:12

"What a Friend We Have in Jesus" by Joseph Medlicott Scriven (1819–1886)

What a Friend we have in Jesus, All our sins and griefs to bear! What a privilege to carry Everything to God in Prayer! O what peace we often forfeit, O what needless pain we bear, All because we do not carry Everything to God in prayer! / Have we trials and temptations? Is there trouble anywhere? We should never be discouraged—Take it to the

Lord in prayer. Can we find a friend so faithful Who will all our sorrows share? Jesus knows our every weakness—Take it to the Lord in prayer. / Are we weak and heavy-laden, Cumbered with a load of care? Precious Savior, still our refuge—Take it to the Lord in prayer. Do thy friends despise, forsake Thee? Take it to the Lord in prayer; In His arms He'll take and shield thee—Thou wilt find a solace there.

BEREAVEMENT: LOSING ONE'S MATE

Job 12:10; 13:15; 14:5; 23:10; Psalm 145:18; 146:9; Isaiah 54:4–5; Jeremiah 29:11; Galatians 6:2; Revelation 21:4

COMFORT

Psalm 9:9; 18:2; 22:24; 27:14; 37:24, 39; 46:1–3; 55:22; 138:7; Lamentations 3:31–33; Nahum 1:7; Matthew 11:28; John 16:33; 2 Corinthians 1:5

"All the Way My Savior Leads Me" by Fanny Jane Crosby (1820–1915)

All the way my Savior leads me—What have I to ask beside? Can I doubt His tender mercy, Who through life has been my Guide? Heav'nly peace, divinest comfort, Here by faith in Him to dwell! For I know whate'er befall me, Jesus doeth all things well; For I know whate'er befall me, Jesus doeth all things well. / All the way my Savior leads me—Cheers each winding path I tread, Gives me grace for ev'ry trial, Feeds me with the living bread. Though my weary steps may falter And my soul athirst may be, Gushing from the Rock before me, Lo! A spring of joy I see; Gushing from the Rock before me, Lo! a spring of joy I see. / All the way my Savior leads me; Oh, the fullness of His love! Perfect rest to me is promised In my Father's house above: When my spirit, clothed immortal, Wings its flight to realms of day, This my song through endless ages: Jesus led me all the way; This my song through endless ages: Jesus led me all the way.

COMFORT FOR ELDERLY

Isaiah 41:10; 46:4; Philippians 4:13; 1 Timothy 5:3, 8; James 1:27

"O Love Divine, That Stooped to Share" by Oliver Wendell Holmes (1809–1894)

O Love Divine, that stooped to share Our sharpest pang, our bitterest tear, On Thee we cast each earthborn care; We smile at pain while Thou art near. Though long the weary way we tread, And sorrow crown, each lingering year, No path we shun, no darkness dread, Our hearts still whispering, "Thou art near!" When drooping pleasure turns to grief, And trembling faith is changed to fear, The murmuring wind, the quivering leaf Shall softly tell us Thou art near! On Thee we fling our burdening woe, O Love divine, forever dear, Content to suffer while we know, Living and dying, Thou art near!

COURAGE

2 Kings 6:16; Psalm 27:14; 31:24; 37:3, 28; Isaiah 40:29; 43:1; Philippians 4:12–13

"God Will Take Care of You" by Civilla Durfee Martin (1866–1948)

Be not dismayed whate'er betide, God will take care of you; Beneath His wings of love abide, God will take care of you. / Through days of toil when heart doth fail, God will take care of you; When dangers fierce your path assail, God will take care of you. / All you may need He will provide, God will take care of you; Nothing you ask will be denied, God will take care of you. / No matter what may be the test, God will take care of you; Lean, weary one, upon His breast, God will take care of you.

DEATH, FEAR OF

Psalm 23:4; 48:14; 49:15; 73:26; Proverbs 14:32; Isaiah 25:8; John 8:51; 11:25; 14:1–3; Romans 8:38–39; 1 Corinthians 2:9–10; 15:54–55; 2 Corinthians 4:16; 5:1; Philippians 1:21; 3:20–21; 2 Timothy 1:10

"Abide with Me" by Henry Francis Lyte (1793–1847)

Abide with me—fast falls the eventide! The darkness deepens—Lord, with me abide! When other helpers fail and comforts flee, Help of the helpless, O abide with me. / Swift to its close ebbs out life's little day, Earth's joys grow dim, its glories pass away; Change and decaying all around I see— O Thou who changest not, abide with me. / I need Thy presence every passing hour—What but Thy grace can foil the tempter's power? Who like Thyself my guide and stay can be? Through cloud and sunshine, O abide with me. / I fear no foe with Thee at hand to bless, Ills have no weight and tears no bitterness; Where is death's sting? where, grave, thy victory? I triumph still if Thou abide with me. / Hold Thou Thy Word before my closing eyes, Shine through the gloom and point me to the skies; Heav'n's morning breaks and earth's vain shadows flee—In life, in death, O Lord, abide with me.

"Peace, Perfect Peace" by Edward Henry Bickersteth (1825–1906)

Peace, perfect peace—with sorrows surging round? On Jesus' bosom naught but calm is found. / Peace, perfect peace—our future all unknown? Jesus we know, and He is on the throne. / Peace, perfect peace—death shadowing us

and ours? Jesus has vanquished death and all its powers. /
It is enough: earth's struggles soon shall cease, And Jesus,
call us to heav'n's perfect peace.

DEPRESSION, DISCOURAGEMENT

Psalm 27:13–14; 38:3–4, 6, 8; 51:3, 12; Isaiah 41:10; Matthew
11:28–30; Mark 11:25; Philippians 4:13; 1 Thessalonians 5:18;
2 Timothy 1:7

"How Firm a Foundation" by "K" in Rippon's Selection of
Hymns (1787)

How firm a foundation, ye saints of the Lord, Is laid for your
faith in His excellent Word! What more can He say than to
you He hath said, To you who for refuge to Jesus have fled?
/ "Fear not, I am with thee; O be not dismayed, For I am thy
God, and will still give thee aid; I'll strengthen thee, help
thee, and cause thee to stand, Upheld by My righteous,
omnipotent hand. / "When through the deep waters I call
thee to go, The rivers of woe shall not thee overflow; For I
will be with thee thy troubles to bless, And sanctify to thee
thy deepest distress. / "When through fiery trials thy path-
ways shall lie, My grace, all-sufficient, shall be thy supply;
Thy flame shall not hurt thee; I only design Thy dross to
consume, and thy gold to refine. / The soul that on Jesus
still leans for repose, I will not, I will not desert to his foes;
That soul, though all hell should endeavor to shake, I'll
never, no, never, no, never forsake."

FAITH

Mark 11:22–23; 1 Corinthians 16:13; 2 Corinthians 5:7; Galatians
2:20; 3:26; 5:22; Ephesians 2:8; 3:17–19; Colossians 2:6–7;
2 Timothy 3:14–15; Hebrews 11:1, 6; 12:1–2; James 1:5–6

"He Giveth More Grace" by Annie Johnson Flint (1866–1932)
He giveth more grace when the burden grows greater; He sendeth more strength when the labors increase. To added affliction He addeth His mercy; To multiplied trials, His mutiplied peace. / [chorus] His love has no limit; His grace has no measure; His pow'r has no boundary known unto men. For out of His infinite riches in Jesus, He giveth, and giveth, and giveth again! / When we have exhausted our store of endurance, When our strength has failed the day is half done, When we reach the end of our hoarded resources, Our Father's full giving is only begun.

"Jesus Loves Me" by Anna Bartlett Warner (1820–1915)
Jesus loves me! This I know, For the Bible tells me so; Little ones to Him belong, They are weak but He is strong. / [chorus] Yes, Jesus loves me! Yes, Jesus loves me! Yes, Jesus loves me! The Bible tells me so. / Jesus loves me! He who died Heaven's gate to open wide; He will wash away my sin, Let His little child come in. / Jesus Loves me! He will stay Close beside me all the way; Thou hast bled and died for me, I will henceforth live for Thee.

FEAR (SEE ALSO ANXIETY AND WORRY)

Psalm 27:1; 34:4; 46:1; 91:4–6; Proverbs 1:33; 3:25–26; Isaiah 35:4; 41:10; 43:2; John 14:27; Romans 8:10; 2 Timothy 1:7; Hebrews 13:5–6; 1 John 4:18

"'Tis So Sweet to Trust in Jesus" by Louisa M. R. Stead (1850–1917)
'Tis so sweet to trust in Jesus, Just to take Him at His word, Just to rest upon His promise, Just to know "Thus saith the Lord." / Yes, 'tis sweet to trust in Jesus, Just from sin and self to cease, Just from Jesus simply taking Life and rest and joy and peace. / I'm so glad I learned to trust Him, Precious Jesus, Savior, Friend; And I know that He is with me, Will be with me to the end.

HEALING

Psalm 66:18; Matthew 18:19; 2 Corinthians 12:7–9; James 1:6;
5:13–16

"Have Thine Own Way, Lord!" by Adelaide Addison Pollard
(1862–1934)

Have Thine own way, Lord! Have Thine own way! Thou art
the Potter; I am the clay. Mold me and make me after Thy
will, While I am waiting, yielded and still. / Have Thine own
way, Lord! Have Thine own way! Search me and try me,
Master, today! Whiter than snow, Lord, wash me just now,
As in Thy presence humbly I bow. / Have Thine own way,
Lord! Have Thine own way! Wounded and weary, help me
I pray! Power, all power, surely is Thine! Touch me and heal
me, Savior divine! / Have Thine own way, Lord! Have thine
own way! Hold o'er my being absolute sway! Fill with Thy
spirit till all shall see Christ only, always, living in me!

HEAVEN

1 Corinthians 15:55, 57; 2 Corinthians 5:6, 8; Philippians 1:21,
23–24; 1 John 3:2; Revelation 21:2, 4

HOPE

Psalm 27:13–14; 31:24; 42:11; 60:5; 71:5; Jeremiah 17:7; Romans
15:13; 2 Corinthians 4:8–10; Colossians 1:5, 27; Titus 2:13; 1 Peter
1:3, 13, 21

"Near to the Heart of God" by Cleland Boyd McAfee
(1866–1944)

There is a place of quiet rest Near to the heart of God, A
place where sin cannot molest, Near to the heart of God. O
Jesus, blest Redeemer, Sent from the heart of God, Hold us
who wait before Thee Near to the heart of God.

"Turn Your Eyes Upon Jesus" by Helen Howarth Lemmel (1864–1961)

O soul, are you weary and troubled? No light in the darkness you see? There's light for a look at the Savior, And life more abundant and free. / [chorus] Turn your eyes upon Jesus, Look full in His wonderful face, And the things of earth will grow strangely dim In the light of His glory and grace. / Through death into life everlasting He passed, and we follow Him there; Over us sin no more hath dominion—For more than conquerors we are! / His Word shall not fail you—He promised; Believe Him and all will be well: Then go to a world that is dying, His perfect salvation to tell!

ILLNESS, SICKNESS (SEE ALSO SUFFERING)

Exodus 23:25; Isaiah 53:5; Jeremiah 17:14; 30:17; Matthew 4:23–24; 9:6–7, 28–30; Romans 8:28; 2 Corinthians 12:9–10; Philippians 4:6–7; 1 Thessalonians 5:18; James 5:13–16; 1 Peter 2:24

"Under His Wings I Am Safely Abiding" by William Orcutt Cushing (1823–1902)

Under His wings I am safely abiding; Though the night deepens and tempests are wild, Still I can trust Him, I know He will keep me; He has redeemed me and I am His child. / Under His wings, under His wings, Who from His love can sever? Under His wings my soul shall abide, Safely abide forever. / Under His wings, what a refuge in sorrow! How the heart yearningly turns to His rest! Often when earth has no balm for my healing, There I find comfort and there I am blest. / Under His wings, O what precious enjoyment! There will I hide till life's trials are o'er; Sheltered, protected, no evil can harm me; Resting in Jesus I'm safe evermore.

PEACE

Psalm 4:8; 119:165; Isaiah 26:3; 48:18; Luke 1:76–79; John 14:27; 16:33; Romans 5:1; 8:6; 14:17, 19; 1 Corinthians 14:33; Ephesians 2:14; Philippians 4:6–7; Colossians 3:15

"It Is Well With My Soul" by Horatio Gates Spafford (1828–1888)

When peace like a river attendeth my way, When sorrows like sea-billows roll; Whatever my lot, Thou hast taught me to say, "It is well, it is well with my soul." / [chorus] It is well with my soul, It is well, it is well with my soul. / Though Satan should buffet, tho' trials should come, Let this blest assurance control, That Christ has regarded my helpless estate, And hath shed His own blood for my soul.

"Like a River Glorious" by Francis Ridley Havergal (1836–1879)

Like a river glorious Is God's perfect peace, Over all victorious In its bright increase; Perfect, yet it floweth Fuller ev'ry day, Perfect, yet it growth Deeper all the way. / Stayed upon Jehovah, Hearts are fully blest—Finding as He promised Perfect peace and rest. / Hidden in the hollow Of His blessed hand, Never foe can follow, Never traitor stand; Not a surge of worry, Not a shade of care, Not a blast of hurry Touch the spirit there. / Every joy or trial Falleth from above, Traced upon our dial By the son of love; We may trust Him fully All for us to do—They who trust Him wholly Find Him wholly true.

STRENGTH

Job 5:19; 8:20–21; Psalm 9:9; 18:2, 28; 22:24; 31:23; 32:7; 34:19; 37:24, 39; 42:11; 68:13; 71:20; 73:26; 91:10–11; 126:5–6; 138:7; 146:8; Lamentations 3:31–33; Micah 7:8–9; John 16:33

"Day by Day" by Carolina Sandell Berg (1832–1903)
Day by day and with each passing moment, Strength I find to meet my trials here; Trusting in my Father's wise bestowment, I've no cause for worry or fear. He whose heart is kind beyond all measure Gives unto each day what He deems best— Lovingly, its part of pain and pleasure, Mingling toil with peace and rest. / Ev'ry day the Lord Himself is near me With a special mercy for each hour; All my cares He fain would bear, and cheer me, He whose name is Counselor and Pow'r. The protection of His child and treasure Is a charge that on Himself He laid; "As thy days, thy strength shall be in measure," This the pledge to me He made. / Help me then in ev'ry tribulation So to trust Thy promises, O Lord, That I lose not faith's sweet consolation Offered me within Thy holy Word. Help me, Lord, when toil and trouble meeting, E'er to take, as from a father's hand, One by one, the days, the moments fleeting, Til I reach the promised land.

SUFFERING

Isaiah 43:2; John 14:1; 16:33; Romans 5:3–5; 8:28–29, 35–39; 2 Corinthians 1:3–10; James 1:2–3, 12; 1 Peter 4:12–13, 16–17; Revelation 21:4

"Be Still My Soul" by Katharina Amalia von Schlegel (1697–?)
Be still, my soul! The Lord is on thy side; Bear patiently the cross of grief or pain; Leave to thy God to order and provide; In every change He faithful will remain. Be still my soul! Thy best, thy heavenly Friend Through thorny ways leads us to a joyful end. / Be still, my soul! Thy God doth undertake To guide the future as He has the past. Thy hope, thy confidence let nothing shake; All now mysterious shall be bright at last. Be still, my soul! The waves and winds still know His voice who ruled them while He dwelt below. / Be

still, my soul! The hour is hastening on When we shall be forever with the Lord, When disappointment, grief, and fear are gone, Sorrow forgot, love's purest joys restored. Be still, my soul! When change and tears are past, All safe and blessed we shall meet at last.

SUICIDE

Job 5:15; Psalm 34:1, 7; 91:1, 11–12, 15–16; John 10:10; Hebrews 4:16

TRUST

Psalm 37:3–5; 40:4; 46:1–2; 84:11–12; 125:1; Proverbs 3:5–6; Nahum 1:7; Matthew 6:31–32; Luke 12:32; 1 Peter 5:7

"How Sweet the Name of Jesus Sounds" by John Newton (1725–1807)

How sweet the name of Jesus sounds In a believer's ear! It soothes his sorrows, heals his wounds, And drives away his fear. / It makes the wounded spirit whole And calms the troubled breast; 'Tis manna to the hungry soul And to the weary, rest. / Dear name! The rock on which I build, My shield and hiding place; My never-failing treasure, filled With boundless stores of grace! / Jesus, my Shepherd, Brother, Friend, My Prophet, Priest, and King, My Lord, my Life, my Way, my End, Accept the praise I bring. / Till then I would Thy love proclaim With ev'ry fleeting breath; And may the music of Thy name Refresh my soul in death.

Recommended Resources

ASSOCIATIONS, ORGANIZATIONS, AND FOUNDATIONS

ALZHEIMER'S DISEASE

Alzheimer's Association; 919 N. Michigan Ave., Suite 1100, Chicago, IL 60611-1676; 800-272-3900, 312-335-8700; www.alz.org.

Alzheimer's Disease Education and Referral Center (a service of the National Institute on Aging); P.O. Box 8250, Silver Spring, MD 20907-8250; 800-438-4380; www.alzheimers.org.

National Institute of Neurological Disorders and Stroke; P.O. Box 5801, Bethesda, MD 20824; 800-352-9424, 301-496-5751; www.ninds.nih.gov.

National Institute on Aging; 31 Center Dr., MSC 2292, Building 31, Room 5C27, Bethesda, MD 20892; 301-496-1752; www.nih.gov/nia.

AMERICAN ASSOCIATION FOR RETIRED PERSONS

601 E St. N.W., Washington, DC 20049; 800-424-3410; www.aarp.org.

AMERICAN MEDICAL ASSOCIATION HEADQUARTERS

515 N. State St., Chicago, IL 60610; 312-464-5000; www.ama-assn.org.

CANCER

American Cancer Society; 1599 Clifton Rd. N.E., Atlanta, GA 30329; 800-227-2345, 404-320-3333; www.cancer.org.

Cancer Care, Inc., National Office; 275 7th Ave., New York, NY 10001; 800-813-4673, 212-302-2400; www.cancercare.org.

CancerEducation.com, Inc.; 730 5th Avenue, New York, NY 10019; 212-727-0427; www.cancereducation.com.

CancerGuide, a cancer information page; www.cancerguide.org.

CancerNet; www.cancernet.nci.nih.gov.

Memorial Sloan-Kettering Cancer Center, main campus, Manhattan's Upper East Side; 1275 York Ave., New York, NY 10021; 800-422-6237; www.mskcc.org.

National Cancer Institute; Room 10A31 Center Dr., MSC 2580, Bethesda, MD 20892; 800-4-CANCER; www.nci.nih.gov.

National Coalition for Cancer Survivorship; 1010 Wayne Ave., Suite 770, Silver Spring, MD 20910-5600; 877-622-7937 (toll free); www.cansearch.org.

University of Pennsylvannia Oncolink; www.oncolink.upenn.edu.

The University of Texas M. D. Anderson Cancer Center; 1515 Holcombe Blvd, Houston, TX 77030; 800-392-1611, 713-792-6161; www.mdanderson.org.

CAREGIVERS

National Family Caregivers Association; 10400 Connecticut Ave., #500, Kensington, MD 20895-3944; 800-896-3650; www.nfcacares.org.

CHILDREN

Make-A-Wish Foundation; 3550 N. Central Ave., Suite 300, Phoenix, AZ 85012; 800-722-9474; www.wish.org.

The National Children's Cancer Society; 1015 Locust, Suite 600, St. Louis, MO 63101; 800-532-6459; www.children-cancer.com.

St. Jude Children's Research Hospital; 501 St. Jude Place, Memphis, TN 38105; 800-877-5833, 901-522-9733; www.stjude.org.

CHRISTIAN MEDICAL AND DENTAL ASSOCIATIONS

P.O. Box 7500, Bristol, TN 37621; 888-230-2637, 423-844-1000; www.cmds.org.

Death and dying

Americans for Better Care of the Dying; 4125 Albemarle St. N.W., Suite 210, Washington, DC 20016; 202-895-9485; www.abcd-caring.org.

Dr. Ira Byock Web site, www.dyingwell.org.

Disabilities

Christopher Reeve Paralysis Foundation; 500 Morris Ave., Springfield, NJ 07081; 800-225-0292; www.apacure.com.

Joni and Friends, The Disability Outreach of Joni Eareckson Tada; P.O. Box 3333, Agoura Hills, CA 91376; 818-707-5664; www.joniandfriends.org.

Elder care

Information on www.elderweb.com.

Funerals

See information from AARP above.

General health web sites

www.intelihealth.com.
www.healthgate.com.

Hospice

American Academy of Hospice and Palliative Medicine; 4700 W. Lake Ave., Glenview, IL 60025-1485; 847-375-4712; www.aahpm.org.

American Hospice Foundation; 2120 L St. N.W., Suite 200, Washington, DC 20037; 202-223-0204; www.americanhospice.org.

Children's Hospice International; 2202 Mt. Vernon Ave., Suite 3C, Alexandria, VA 22301; 800-242-4453, 703-684-0330; www.chionline.org.

Hospice and Palliative Nurses Association; www.hpna.org.

Hospice Association of America; 228 7th St., S.E., Washington, DC 20003; 202-546-479; www.nahc.org/haa.

Hospice Foundation of America; 2001 S St. N.W., Suite 300, Washington DC 20009; 800-854-3402; www.hospicefoundation.org.

National Hospice and Palliative Care Organization; 1700 Diagonal Rd., Suite 300, Alexandria, VA 22314; 800-658-8898, 703-837-1500; www.nhpco.org.

JOB ACCOMMODATION NETWORK (JAN)

West Virginia University, P.O. Box 6080, Morgantown, WV, 26506, 800-526-7234 (V/TTY); janweb.icdi.wvu.edu.

LOU GEHRIG'S DISEASE

The Amyotrophic Lateral Sclerosis Association, National Office; 27001 Agoura Rd., Suite 150, Calabasas Hills, CA 91301-5104; 800-782-4747, 818-880-9007; www.alsa.org. Doctor's guide; www.pslgroup.com/ALS.HTM.

MULTIPLE SCLEROSIS

The National Multiple Sclerosis Society; 733 Third Ave., New York, NY 10017; 800-344-4867; www.nmss.org.

NATIONAL CENTER FOR COMPLEMENTARY AND ALTERNATIVE MEDICINE

NCCAM Clearinghouse, P.O. Box 8218, Silver Spring, MD 20907-8218; 888-644-6226; www.nccam.nih.gov.

NATIONAL INSTITUTES OF HEALTH (NIH)

Bethesda, MD 20892; www.nih.gov.

NATIONAL INSTITUTE OF MENTAL HEALTH (NIMH)

Public Inquiries, 6001 Executive Blvd., Room 8184, MSC 9663, Bethesda, MD 20892-9663; 301-443-4513; www.nimh.nih.org.

NATIONAL INSTITUTE OF NEUROLOGICAL DISORDERS AND STROKE

P.O. Box 5801, Bethesda, MD 20824; 800-352-9424, 301-496-5751; www.ninds.nih.gov.

NATIONAL LIBRARY OF MEDICINE

8600 Rockville Pike, Bethesda, MD 20894; www.nlm.nih.gov.

PAIN

American Academy of Pain Management; 13947 Mono Way, #A, Sonora CA 95370; 209-533-9744; www.aapainmanage.org.

American Pain Foundation; 111 S. Calvert St., Suite 2700, Baltimore, MD 21202; www.painfoundation.org.

American Pain Society; 4700 W. Lake Ave., Glenview, IL 60025; 847-375-4715; www.ampainsoc.org.

Pain.com, an electronic library of information on pain; www.pain.com.

PARKINSON'S DISEASE

The American Parkinson Disease Association, Inc.; 1250 Hylan Blvd., Suite 4B, Staten Island, NY 10305-1946; 800-223-2732, 718-981-8001; www.apdaparkinson.com.

Parkinson's Disease Foundation; 710 W. 168th St., New York, NY 10032-9982; 800-457-6676, 212-923-4700; www.pdf.org.

STEPHEN MINISTRIES

2045 Innerbelt Business Center Dr., St. Louis, MO 63114-5765; 314-428-2600; www.stephenministries.org.

SUICIDE

American Association of Suicidology; 4201 Connecticut Ave. N.W., Suite 408, Washington, DC 20008; 202-237-2280; www.suicidology.org.

U.S. DEPARTMENT OF HEALTH AND HUMAN SERVICES,

200 Independence Ave., S.W., Washington, DC 20201, 877-696-6775 (toll free); www.os.dhhs.gov. (Healthfinder, a free gateway to reliable consumer health information; www.healthfinder.gov.).

WORLD HEALTH ORGANIZATION,

Headquarters Office in Geneva (HQ); Avenue Appia 20, 1211 Geneva 27, Switzerland; (+00 41 22) 791 21 11; www.who.int.

Recommended Reading

CHRISTIAN/INSPIRATIONAL LIVING

Billy Graham Evangelistic Association compilations. *The Billy Graham Christian Worker's Handbook: A Comprehensive Counseling Guide.* Minneapolis, Minn.: World Wide, A Ministry of the Billy Graham Evangelistic Association, 1981.

Burroughs, Jeremiah. *The Rare Jewel of Christian Contentment.* Carlisle, Penn.: Banner of Truth, 1979.

Carmichael, Amy. *A Very Present Help.* Ann Arbor, Mich.: Servant, Vine Books, 1996.

Galli, Mark, and James S. Bell Jr. *The Complete Idiot's Guide to Prayer.* Indianapolis, Ind.: Alpha Books, 1999.

Hurnard, Hannah. *Hinds' Feet on High Places: An Allegory Dramatizing the Journey Each of Us Must Take before We Can Live in "High Places."* Wheaton, Ill.: Tyndale, 1997.

Hybels, Bill. *Too Busy Not to Pray: Slowing Down to Be with God.* Downers Grove, Ill.: InterVarsity, 1998.

LeSourd, Catherine Marshall. *The Inspirational Writings of Catherine Marshall: Something More and a Closer Walk.* New York: Inspirational Press, 1990.

Lewis, C. S. *Mere Christianity.* New York: Collier Books, Macmillan, 1952.

MacArthur, John. *The Ultimate Priority: On Worship.* Chicago, Ill.: Moody, 1983.

Moore, Pamela Rosewell. *The Five Silent Years of Corrie ten Boom.* Grand Rapids, Mich.: Zondervan, 1986.

Morgan, Richard L. *From Grim to Green Pastures: Meditations for the Sick and Their Caregivers.* Nashville, Tenn.: Upper Room Books, 1994.

Ogilvie, Lloyd. *A Future and a Hope.* Dallas, Tex.: Word Publishing, 1988.

Palmer, Bernard. *Nothing Is Impossible: The Eugene Clark Story.* Chicago, Ill.: Moody, 1979.

ten Boom, Corrie. *Jesus Is Victor.* Grand Rapids, Mich.: Revell, 1985.

Wiersbe, Warren W. *Be Joyful: Even When Things Go Wrong, You Can Have Joy.* Wheaton, Ill.: SP Publications, Victor Books, 1974.

DEATH AND DYING

Byock, Ira, M.D. *Dying Well: The Prospect for Growth at the End of Life.* New York: Putnam Publishing Group, Riverhead Books, 1997.

Graham, Billy. *Death and the Life After.* Dallas, Tex.: Word Publishing, 1987.

Lutzer, Erin W. *One Minute After You Die: A Preview of Your Final Destination.* Chicago, Ill.: Moody, 1997.

Orr, Robert D., M.D.; David L. Schiedermayer, M.D.; and David B. Biebel, D.Min. *Life and Death Decisions: Help in Making Tough Choices about Bioethical Issues.* Colorado Springs, Colo.: Navpress, 1990.

Satterly, Lamont. *If I Should Wake Before I Die: Healing Words for Dying People.* Maple Glen, Penn.: Search Foundation, 1997.

Taylor, Rick. *When Life Is Changed Forever by the Death of Someone Near.* Eugene, Ore.: Harvest House, 1992.

Vanauken, Sheldon. *A Severe Mercy.* New York: HarperCollins, 1985.

Watson, David. *Fear No Evil: One Man Deals with Terminal Illness.* Wheaton, Ill.: Shaw Publishers, 1992.

Welsey, Gil, and Debbie Welsey. *Facing Death As a Couple.* With host Dennis Rainey. Little Rock, Ark.: A Family Life Today audio series, 1994.

EUTHANASIA AND PHYSICIAN-ASSISTED SUICIDE

Christian Medical and Dental Society. *The Battle for Life (An Educational Resource Kit in the Fight Against Physician-Assisted Suicide by Christian Doctors)*. Bristol, Tenn.: 1995.

Larson, Edward J., and Darrel W. Amundson. *A Different Death: Euthanasia and the Christian Tradition*. Downers Grove, Ill.: InterVarsity, 1998.

Pedreira, Frank, M.D. *A Doctor's Prescription for Life: A Christian Doctor's Examination of Life's Most Challenging Decisions*. Pittsburgh, Penn.: CeShore Publishing, 1999.

Willke, J. C., M.D.; with Frederic Wertham, M.D.; Cathleen Cleaver, J.D.; Edward Grant, J.D.; and Mark Rothe, J.D. *Assisted Suicide and Euthanasia: Past and Present*. Cincinnati, Ohio: Hayes, 1998.

GOD

Anders, Max. *God: Knowing Our Creator*. Nashville, Tenn.: Thomas Nelson, 1995.

Lewis, C. S. *Miracles: A Preliminary Study*. New York: Macmillan, 1947.

Pink, Arthur W. *The Attributes of God*. Grand Rapids, Mich.: Baker Books, 1975.

GRIEF

Atchison, Liam, and Precious Atchison. *Grief*. Colorado Springs, Colo.: NavPress, 1993.

Kinnaman, Gary. *My Companion through Grief: Comfort for Your Darkest Hours*. Ann Arbor, Mich.: Servant, Vine Books, 1996.

Lewis, C. S. *A Grief Observed*. New York: HarperSan Francisco, 1989.

HEAVEN

Bayly, Joseph. *Heaven*. Elgin, Ill.: David C. Cook, 1977.

Kreeft, Peter. *Heaven: The Heart's Deepest Longing*. San Francisco, Calif.: Ignatius Press, 1989.

MacArthur, John F. *The Glory of Heaven: The Truth about Heaven, Angels, and Eternal Life*. Wheaton, Ill.: Crossway Books, 1996.

Moody, Dwight L. *Heaven*. Chicago, Ill.: Moody, 1995.

Sanders, J. Oswald. *Heaven Better by Far: Answers to Questions about the Believer's Final Hope*. Grand Rapids, Mich.: Discovery House Publishers, 1993.

Tada, Joni Eareckson. *Heaven: Your Real Home*. Grand Rapids, Mich.: Zondervan, 1995.

SERIOUS ILLNESS

Anderson, Greg. *Fifty Essential Things to Do When the Doctor Says It's Cancer*. New York: NAL-Dutton, Plume, 1993.

Atkins, Marguerite Henry. *Also My Journey: A Personal Story of Alzheimer's*. Wilton, England: Morehouse-Barlow, 1985.

Davis, Robert. *My Journey into Alzheimer's Disease*. Wheaton, Ill.: Tyndale, 1989.

Harpham, Wendy Schlessel, M.D. *After Cancer: A Guide to Your New Life*. New York: HarperCollins, HarperPerennial, 1995.

Harpham, Wendy Schlessel, M.D. *Diagnosis Cancer: Your Guide through the First Few Months*. New York: Norton, 1992.

Harwell, Amy, with Kristine Tomasik. *When Your Friend Gets Cancer: How You Can Help*. Wheaton, Ill.: Shaw Publishers, 1987.

Hawkins, Don, Daniel L. Koppersmith, M.D., and Ginger Koppersmith. *When Cancer Comes: Mobilizing Physical, Emotional, and Spiritual Resources to Combat One of Life's Most Dreaded Diseases*. Chicago, Ill.: Moody, 1993.

Klein, Allen. *The Healing Power of Humor: The Techniques for Getting through Loss, Setbacks, Upsets, Disappointments, Difficulties, Trials, Tribulations, and All That Not-So-Funny Stuff*. Los Angeles: JP Tarcher-Putnam, 1989.

Kolf, June Cerza. *Comfort and Care for the Critically Ill*. Grand Rapids, Mich.: Baker Books, 1993.

Lynn, Joanne, M.D., and Joan Harrold, M.D. *Handbook for Mortals: Guidance for People Facing Serious Illness*. New York: Oxford University Press, 1999.

McFarlane, Rodger, and Philip Bashe. *The Complete Bedside Companion: No-Nonsense Advice on Caring for the Seriously Ill*. New York: Simon and Schuster, 1998.

Morra, Marion, and Eve Potts. *Choices: Realistic Alternatives in Cancer Treatment*. 2nd ed. New York: Avon, 1987.

Moster, Mary Beth. *Living with Cancer: When Cancer Strikes You or Someone You Love, You Can Face Life with Hope, Courage, and Peace*. Wheaton, Ill.: Tyndale, 1979.

National Coalition for Cancer Survivorship. *Charting the Journey: An Almanac of Practical Resources for Cancer Survivors*. Edited by Fitzhugh Mullan, M.D.; Barbara Hoffman, J.D.; and the editors of Consumer Reports Books. Mount Vernon, N.Y.: Consumers Union, 1990.

Pomeroy, DanaRae. *When Someone You Love Has Cancer*. New York: Berkley Books, 1996.

Shelly, Judith Allen. *Spiritual Care: A Guide for Caregivers*. Downers Grove, Ill.: InterVarsity, 2000.

Tada, Joni Eareckson. *The Life and Death Dilemma: Families Facing Health Care Choices*. Grand Rapids, Mich.: Zondervan, 1995.

SUFFERING AND PAIN

Barnes, M. Craig. *When God Interrupts: Finding New Life through Unwanted Change*. Downers Grove, Ill.: InterVarsity, 1996.

Biebel, David B. *If God Is So Good, Why Do I Hurt So Bad? An Understanding Look at the Journey from Pain to Wholeness*. Colorado Springs, Colo.: Navpress, 1991.

Billheimer, Paul E. *Don't Waste Your Sorrows: New Insight into God's Eternal Purpose for Each Christian in the Midst of Life's Greatest Adversities*. Minneapolis, Minn.: Bethany House, 1977.

Bonhoeffer, Dietrich. *Meditations on the Cross*. English Translation. Louisville, Ky.: Westminster John Knox, 1998.

Dobson, Dr. James. *When God Doesn't Make Sense*. Wheaton, Ill.: Tyndale, 1993.

Elliot, Elisabeth. *A Path through Suffering: Discovering the Relationship between God's Mercy and Our Pain*. Ann Arbor, Mich.: Servant, Vine Books, 1990.

Graham, Billy. *Hope for the Troubled Heart*. New York: Bantam, 1993.

Johnson, Barbara. *Stick a Geranium in Your Hat and Be Happy: Pain Is Inevitable but Misery Is Optional*. Dallas, Tex.: Word Publishing, 1990.

Jones, James. *Why Do People Suffer?* Oxford, England: Lion Publishing, 1993.

Kreeft, Peter. *Making Sense out of Suffering*. New York: Phoenix Press, Walker and Co., 1987.

Lewis, C. S. *The Problem of Pain*. New York: Macmillan, 1962.

Mayhall, Carole. *Help Lord: My Whole Life Hurts*. Colorado Springs, Colo.: Navpress, 1988.

Rankin, Peg. *Yet Will I Trust Him*. Glendale, Calif.: Regal Books, 1980.

Sproul, R. C. *Surprised by Suffering*. Wheaton, Ill.: Tyndale, 1989.

Wiersbe, Warren W. *The Bumps Are What You Climb On: Encouragement for Difficult Days*. Grand Rapids, Mich.: Baker Books, 1980.

Wiersbe, Warren W., comp. *Classic Sermons on Suffering*. Grand Rapids, Mich.: Kregel, 1984.

Yancey, Philip. *Where Is God When It Hurts?* Grand Rapids, Mich.: Zondervan, 1977.

CHAPTER 1

1. Interview with Mary Raymer, M.S.W., A.C.S.W. Raymer is the director of Raymer Psychotherapy and Consultation Services, P.C., and Social Work Section Leader for the National Hospice and Palliative Care Organization in Arlington, Virginia. For twenty-two years she has served in a variety of clinical and administrative roles in hospice care. In her private practice she specializes in chronic and terminal illness, depression, and complicated grief. She is an educator, consultant, therapist, and published author who in 1997 received the Lifetime Achievement Award from the Michigan Hospice Organization for her role in promoting hospice statewide. She lectures and consults nationally and internationally on palliative care issues and is currently the project leader for community awareness for a $450,000 Robert Wood Johnson grant to improve end-of-life care in the state of Michigan.

2. Interview with Dr. Daniel Haffey, a licensed clinical psychologist practicing with Westview Psychological Services in Frederick, Maryland. Dr. Haffey treats adolescents and adults and has a special interest in grief and bereavement issues as well as the integration of Christian faith and psychology.

3. Interview with Elise C. Kohn, M.D., Chief, Molecular Signaling Section, Laboratory of Pathology, at the National Cancer Institute.

4. *Encyclopedia of Death*, eds. Robert and Beatrice Kastenbaum (Phoenix, Ariz: Oryx Press, 1989), 127.

5. Cited in John Costello, R.M.N., R.G.N., R.N.T., M.Ed., "Helping Relatives Cope with the Grieving Process," *Professional Nurse* 11, no. 2 (November 1995): 89.

6. C. S. Lewis, *A Grief Observed* (San Franciso: HarperSanFrancisco, 1961), 69.

7. Wendy Schlessel Harpham, M.D., *Diagnosis Cancer: Your Guide through the First Few Months* (New York: W.W. Norton and Company, 1992), 81.

8. Kastenbaum, *Encyclopedia of Death*, 127–8.

9. Irene Pollin, M.S.W., with Susan K. Galant, *Taking Charge: Overcoming the Challenges of Long-Term Illness* (New York: Times Books, 1994), 97.

10. Judy Harrison, Peter Maguire, Tracey Ibbotson, Rhona Macleod, and Penelope Hopwood, "Concerns, Confiding, and Psychiatric Disorder in Newly Diagnosed Cancer Patients," *Psycho-Oncology* 3 (1994): 173–9.

11. *Charting the Journey: An Almanac of Practical Resources for Cancer Survivors*, eds. Fitzhugh Mullan, M.D., Barbara Hoffman, J.D., and the editors of *Consumer Reports Books* (Mount Vernon, N.Y.: Consumers Union of United States, Inc., 1990), 145–59.

CHAPTER 2

1. Max Anders, *God: Knowing Our Creator* (Nashville, Tenn.: Thomas Nelson Publishers, 1995), 23.

2. Interview with Reverend Mark Tindle, Associate Pastor of Seneca Creek Community Church in Germantown, Maryland.

3. Christine Weaver Hunley, M.D. lives in Nashville, Tennessee, with her husband and two children. She practices pediatrics in Goodlettsville, Tennessee.

4. James Jones, *Why Do People Suffer: The Scandal of Pain in God's World* (Batvia, Ill.: Lion Publishing, 1993), 79–80; 85–6.

5. Daniel R. Mitchum, "The Needless Burden of Worry," *Discipleship Journal* 38 (1987): 46.

6. Irene Pollin, M.S.W., with Susan K. Galant, M.A., *Taking Charge: Overcoming the Challenges of Long-Term Illness* (New York: Times Books, 1994), 88.

7. Ibid., chapter 5.

CHAPTER 3

1. David Watson, *Fear No Evil* (Wheaton, Ill.: Harold Shaw Publishers, 1992), 115–6.

2. Philip Yancey, *Where Is God When It Hurts?* (Grand Rapids, Mich.: Zondervan Books, 1977), 70–1.

3. Bernard Palmer, *Nothing Is Impossible: The Eugene Clark Story* (Chicago, Ill.: Moody Press, 1979), 112.

4. Billy Graham, *Hope for the Troubled Heart* (New York: Bantam Books, 1993), 67–8.

5. Interview with the Reverend Robert E. Steinke, Hospital Chaplain and Director of Pastoral Care at Frederick Memorial Healthcare System, Frederick, Maryland. Rev. Robert Steinke received and maintains his Orders for Ordination and credentials as a licensed Hospital Chaplain through the Conservative Congregational Christian Conference and holds additional certifications as an Addictions Counselor, Mental Health Counselor, Medical Ethicist, and Palliative Care Specialist. He is a standing member of the hospital's Cancer Committee, Medical Ethics Committee, Pain Management Committee, Patient Rights Committee, and Institutional Review Board. He is also a contributing editor for Aspen Publishers, a publisher of health-care training manuals. Many of Rev. Robert Steinke's publications are in use in over three hundred hospitals and health-care institutions throughout the country.

CHAPTER 4

1. Philip Yancey, *Where Is God When It Hurts?* (Grand Rapids, Mich.: Zondervan Publishers, 1977), 42.

2. Peter Kreeft, *Making Sense out of Suffering* (New York: Phoenix Press, 1987), 112–3.

3. Ibid., 242.

4. Margaret Clarkson, *Grace Grows Best in Winter: Help for Those Who Must Suffer* (Grand Rapids, Mich.: Zondervan, 1972), 16–7.

5. This list is compiled from several sources, including: George W. Truett, "The Ministry of Suffering" in *Classic Sermons on Suffering*, comp. Warren W. Wiersbe (Grand Rapids, Mich.: Kregel Publications, 1984), 131–43; Peg Rankin, *Yet I Will Trust Him* (Ventura, Calif.: Regal Books, 1993); Edith Margaret Clarkson, *Grace Grows Best in Winter* (Grand Rapids, Mich.: Zondervan, 1972); and *The Billy Graham Christian Worker's Handbook,* comp. BGEA Spiritual Counseling Department, the Billy Graham Evangelistic Association, 1981.

6. Dietrich Bonhoeffer, *Meditations on the Cross* (Louisville, Ky.: Westminster John Knox, 1998), 42–3.

7. James S. Stewart, "Wearing the Thorns As a Crown," in *Classic Sermons on Suffering,* 96.

8. Pamela Rosewell Moore, *The Five Silent Years of Corrie ten Boom* (Grand Rapids, Mich.: Zondervan, 1986), 156–7.

CHAPTER 5

1. Bernard Palmer, *Nothing Is Impossible: The Eugene Clark Story* (Chicago, Ill.: Moody Press, 1979), 102.

2. Irene Pollin, M.S.W., with Susan K. Galant, M.A., *Taking Charge: Overcoming the Challenges of Long-Term Illness* (New York: Times Books, 1994), 30–1.

3. Glenn and Grace had a role in several television programs on the subject of Alzheimer's disease. Glenn believes that exposure led governor Harry Hughes to appoint him to the Maryland Task Force on Alzheimer's Disease and Related Disorders. As a result, Glenn has become involved in the Adult Day Care movement, the Alzheimer's Association, and the Maryland Gerontology Association. He also acts as consultant to a number of groups seeking to serve the disadvantaged elderly. His participation, together with the work of many others, helped prompt Congress to allocate more money to Alzheimer's disease research. According to the Alzheimer's Disease Association, in 1980 federal funding through the National Institutes of Health for research for Alzheimer's disease was

$13 million. This budget steadily increased to $460 million in 2000, with the largest jump occurring in 1990–1991 from $146 to $229 million. The Association is the leading private funder, having raised more than $100 million since its inception in 1980.

4. Natalie Davis Springarn, *Charting the Journey: An Almanac of Practical Resources for Cancer Survivors,* ed. Fitzhugh Mullan, M.D., Barbara Hoffman, J.D., and the editors of Consumer Reports Books **(FOP)**, 49–53. Springarn is a medical writer based in Washington, D.C., and member of the board of directors of the National Coalition for Cancer Survivorship.

5. Interview with David Stevens, M.D. He serves as Executive Director of the Christian Medical Associations, a movement of Christian doctors that seeks to change the heart of health care.

6. Springarn, *Charting the Journey*, 66–9. An excellent resource to consider is the National Center for Complementary and Alternative Medicine (NCCAM), which is part of the National Institutes for Health. NCCAM conducts and supports basic and applied research and training and disseminates information on complementary and alternative medicine to practitioners and the public. Appendixes B and C list medical resources and information, including how to contact the NCCAM.

7. See appendixes B and C for resources.

8. Wendy Schlessel Harpham, M.D., *Diagnosis Cancer: Your Guide through the First Few Months,* (New York: W.W. Norton and Company, 1992), 68–9.

9. Marguerite Henry Atkins, *Also My Journey: A Personal Story of Alzheimer's* (Wilton, Conn.: Morehouse Barlow Co., Inc., 1985), 70.

10. See appendix B for how to contact JAN. JAN can recommend help for individuals suffering from more than thirty different medical conditions: arthritis, attention deficit disorder, bipolar disorder, brain injury, cancer, cerebral palsy, chronic pain, deafness, diabetes, epilepsy, fibromyalgia, fragrance sensitivity, heart conditions, HIV/AIDS, latex allergies, learning disabilities, lupus, migraine headaches, multiple chemical sensitivity, multiple sclerosis, office workers who use wheelchairs, psychiatric impairments, respiratory problems, sight impairments, sleep disorders, and speech impairment.

11. Interview with Gilbert R. Gonzales, M.D., a neurologist at Memorial Sloan-Kettering Cancer Center in New York. His expertise lies in the management of pain. He studies opiate and other pain-related receptors in the spinal cord and brain, mapping pain receptors and correlating them with patients' reported pain, and investigating new ways to administer pain relievers.

12. Interview with Nancy E. Weissman, 17SSW, LCSW, BCD, a social worker

at the National Cancer Institute. Weissman works in the Genetic Epidemiology Branch, where she has introduced a psychosocial component of support and research to the study of families with a high risk of cancer.

13. Harpham, *Diagnosis Cancer: Your Guide through the First Few Months,* 91–2.

14. Atkins, *Also My Journey: A Personal Story of Alzheimer's,* 138–40.

15. Nancy J. Nordenson, "Praying When Lefe Gets Hard," *Discipleship Journal* 116 (March/April 2000), 32–7.

CHAPTER 6

1. This list is adapted by permission from material developed for Family Life's parenting conference. Copyright 1997, 1993. Campus Crusade for Christ International. All rights reserved.

2. Mike Philips, *Getting More Done in Less Time & Having More Fun Doing It!* (Minneapolis, Minn.: Bethany House Publishers, 1982), 41.

3. Jeremiah Burroughs, *The Rare Jewel of Christian Contentment* (Carlisle, Penn.: Banner of Truth, 1979), 19.

4. Joni Eareckson Tada, "When You Can't Escape: How Can You Learn to Be Content When You're Trapped in a Difficult Situation?" *Discipleship Journal* 7, no. 6 (1 November 1987): 23–6.

5. Warren W. Wiersbe, *Be Joyful* (Wheaton, Ill.: Victor Books, 1974), 134–40.

6. Joni Eareckson Tada, "When You Can't Escape," 26.

7. Interview with Reverend Bruce D. Johnson, senior pastor of Seneca Creek Community Church in Germantown, Maryland. Rev. Bruce Johnson is also president of a consulting firm, Making It Clear Communications. This section has been adapted and reprinted with his permission.

CHAPTER 7

1. Wendy Schlessel Harpham, *Diagnosis Cancer: Your Guide through the First Few Months* (New York: W.W. Norton and Company, 1992), 83.

2. U.S. Department of Health and Human Services, *Taking Time: Support for People with Cancer and the People Who Care about Them* (NIH Publication no. 92-2059, reprinted January 1992), 52.

3. Interview with Dr. Gregg Seckman, senior pastor at Gaithersburg Presbyterian Church in Gaithersburg, Maryland.

4. Interview with Dr. Marlin C. Hardman, associate pastor and minister of pastoral care at McLean Presbyterian Church in McLean, Virginia.

5. Interview with the Reverend Joseph N. Nilsen, former pastoral care coordi-

nator at Staten Island University Hospice in Staten Island, New York.

6. Interview with Reverend Faye Serene, previous Associate Pastor for Youth and Nurture at Gaithersburg Presbyterian Church in Gaithersburg, Maryland.

7. This list was compiled from suggestions by Rev. Robert Grohman, Dr. Marlin C. Hardman, Rev. Joseph Nilsen, Dr. Greg Seckman, Rev. Faye Serene, and Chaplain Robert Steinke.

8. Interview with Rev. Robert Grohman, pastor of Sound Beach Community Church in Sound Beach, New York.

9. This list was compiled from suggestions by Rev. Robert Grohman, Dr. Marlin C. Hardman, Rev. Joseph Nilsen, Dr. Greg Seckman, Rev. Faye Serene, and Chaplain Robert Steinke.

10. This list was compiled from suggestions by Dr. Marlin C. Hardman and David G. Seiler, who both lost their wives to cancer.

11. Rosemary Elsdon, "Spiritual Pain in Dying People: The Nurse's Role" *Professional Nurse* 10, no. 10 (July 1995): 641. Elsdon is a staff nurse at the Salisbury Hospice/Palliative Care Unit, Salisbury District Hospital, Salisbury, England.

12. Amy Harwell with Kristine Tomasik, *When Your Friend Gets Cancer: How You Can Help* (Wheaton, Ill.: Harold Shaw Publishers, 1987), xii.

13. Billy Graham, *Hope for the Troubled Heart* (New York: Bantam Books, 1993), 133.

14. Mark Galli and James S. Bell Jr., *The Complete Idiot's Guide to Prayer* (Indianapolis, Ind.: 1999), 195.

15. This list was compiled from suggestions by Rev. Robert Grohman, Dr. Marlin C. Hardman, Rev. Joseph Nilsen, Dr. Greg Seckman, Rev. Faye Serene, and Chaplain Robert Steinke.

16. John Carmody, *Cancer and Faith* (Mystic, Conn.: Twenty-Third Publications, 1994), 74–5.

CHAPTER 8

1. "Cancer Pain Relief and Palliative Care," *Technical Report Series* 804 (Geneva: World Health Organization, 1990): 11.

2. Katharine G. Baker, D.S.W., L.C.S.W., in *Charting the Journey: An Almanac of Practical Resources for Cancer Survivors,* eds. Fitzhugh Mullan, M.D., Barbara Hoffman, J.D., and the editors of *Consumer Reports Books* (Mount Vernon, N.Y.: Consumers Union of United States, Inc., 1990), 155–7.

3. Hannah Hurnard, *Hinds' Feet on High Places* (Wheaton, Ill.: Tyndale House

Publishers, 1975), 228–9. Used by permission. All rights reserved.

4. Helen Lemmel, "Turn Your Eyes Upon Jesus."

5. Timothy D. Crater, *Study of Revelation* (Reston, Va.: Community Bible Study, 1977), 10. For more details on heaven and assurance of salvation, see chapter 11.

CHAPTER 9

1. Edward J. Larson and Darrel W. Amundsen, *A Different Death: Euthanasia and the Christian Tradition* (Downers Grove, Ill.: InterVarsity Press, 1998), 168, 170. See also James F. Freis, "Aging, Natural Death and the Compression of Morbidity," *New England Journal of Medicine* 303 (1980): 130–5 and Bruce C. Vladeck, "End of Life Care," *Journal of the American Medical Association* 274 (1995): 449.

2. See appendix B for resources for information about euthanasia and physician-assisted suicide.

3. Robert D. Orr, M.D., David L. Schiedermayer, M.D., and David B. Beibel, D.Min., *Life and Death Decisions* (Colorado Springs, Colo.: NavPress, 1990), 152.

4. *American Journal of Psychiatry* 152 (August 1995): 1185–91.

5. Jonathan Imbody, M.Ed., "Killing Isn't Caring: What You Should Know about Physician-Assisted Suicide," from the Christian Medical and Dental Associations' Battle for Life educational kit (Bristol, Tenn.: 1998), 2. See also K. M. Foley, "The Relationship of Pain and Symptom Management to Patient Requests for Physician-Assisted Suicide" in *Pain Symptom Management* 6 (1991): 289–97, cited in *Anesthesiology* 78, no. 2 (February 1993): 359.

6. Interview with Joanne Rohrer-Morton M.S.S., A.C.S.W., L.S.W., who has a private practice in Pennsylvania that focuses on loss, grief, and life transition counseling for individuals and groups. She frequently counsels individuals experiencing complicated grief and loss and has developed and facilitated numerous age-appropriate grief support groups for children and adults coping with the death of a loved one. She also shares her expertise through training and consultation.

7. Virginia F. Sendor with Patrice M. O'Connor, *Hospice and Palliative Care: Questions and Answers* (Lanham, Md.: Scarecrow Press, 1997), 126.

8. From the Christian Medical and Dental Associations. Used by permission.

9. Ira Byock, *Dying Well: The Prospect for Growth at the End of Life* (New York: Riverhead Books, 1997), 245.

10. M. Scott Peck, "Living Is the Mystery," *Newsweek* (10 March 1997).

11. National Hospice and Palliative Care Organization, "Facts and Figures on Hospice Care in America," September 2000. These figures are based on actual patient counts supplied by its member hospices and conservative estimates for other hospice programs.

12. Sendor and O'Connor, *Hospice and Palliative Care,* 106.

13. "Facts and Figures on Hospice Care in America." These figures are based on a public opinion survey of people forty-five years of age and older that was conducted for the National Hospice Foundation in April 1999.

14. Press release, 8 June 1999. In early 2000, the National Hospice Organization changed its name to the National Hospice and Palliative Care Organization to reflect the success that hospice programs had achieved in caring for individuals with advanced illness.

15. Suggestions for initiating discussions about end-of-life care and the list of questions to ask if you are considering hospice care have been adapted from NHPCO publications and are used here by permission.

16. Robert D. Orr, M.D., David L. Schiedermayer, M.D., and David B. Beibel, D.Min., *Life and Death Decisions* (Colorado Springs, Colo.: NavPress, 1990), 195–6. Used by permission.

Chapter 10

1. Robert and Bedrock Kastenbaum, *Encyclopedia of Death* (Phoenix, Ariz.: Oryx Press, 1989), 24.

2. Interview with Major Stuart A. Roop, M.D., a fellow in pulmonary critical care at Walter Reed Army Medical Center in Washington, D.C.

3. Betty Davies, Joanne Chekryn Reimer, Pamela Brown, and Nola Martens, *Fading Away: The Experience of Transition in Families with Terminal Illness* (Amityville, N.Y.: Baywood Publishing Company, 1995), 54.

4. Virginia F. Sendor, with Patrice M. O'Connor, *Hospice and Palliative Care: Questions and Answers* (Lanham, Md.: Scarecrow Press, Inc., 1997), 11.

5. Interview with the Reverend Harold A. Peeders, S.T.M., minister of Holy Trinity Evangelical Lutheran Church In Burlington, New Jersey.

6. Jonathan Gavrin, M.D. and C. Richard Chapman, Ph.D., "Clinical Management of Dying Patients," *Western Journal of Medicine* 163, no. 3 (September 1995): 268–77.

7. Ibid.

8. Ira Byock, M.D., *Dying Well: The Prospect for Growth at the End of Life* (New York: Riverhead Books, 1997), 57.

9. Helen L. Taylor, *The Little Pilgrim's Progress* (Chicago, Ill.: Moody Press, 1977), 256. Used by permission.

CHAPTER 11

1. Joni Eareckson Tada, *Heaven: Your Real Home* (Grand Rapids, Mich: Zondervan Publishing House, 1995), 97.

2. Joseph Bayly, *Heaven* (Elgin, Ill.: Life Journey Books, 1977), n.p.

3. Billy Graham, *Facing Death—and the Life After* (Waco, Tex.: Word Books, 1987), 271–2.

4. Bill Bright, *Have You Heard of the Four Spiritual Laws?* (San Bernardino, Calif.: Campus Crusade for Christ International, 1965).

SUBJECT INDEX

Printed in the United States
by Baker & Taylor Publisher Services